MY LIFE IN
BRASSTOWN

An Appalachian Memoir

MY LIFE IN
BRASSTOWN

An Appalachian Memoir

ELEANOR LAMBERT WILSON

BRIGHT MOUNTAIN BOOKS, INC.
FAIRVIEW. NORTH CAROLINA

DEDICATION

To the families and friends who have blessed my life and work . . .

" . . . a lawyer, asked him [Jesus] a question, to test him. 'Teacher, which is the great commandment in the law?' And he said to him, 'You shall love the Lord your God with all your heart, and with all your soul, and with all your mind. This is the great and first commandment. And a second is like it, You shall love your neighbor as yourself.'"

—*Matthew 22:35–39 (Revised Standard Version)*

ACKNOWLEDGMENTS

To my family, Florence Atwood, John Wilson, Anne Harper, and Daniel Wilson, I give my thanks for their love and support. They took the time to read and agree to my stories about their childhood. My thanks to Nancy Simpson whose writing groups I attended in the early years of my retirement and where I shared many first versions of my stories. I am grateful to my friend Benjamin Kennedy, who read and edited the first version of this sequel story and encouraged me to continue; and to Cynthia Bright, who edited the final version. My sincere thanks to all the staff at the Folk School Gift Shop and in the community who begged me to write a "sequel story" to *My Journey to Appalachia*.

CONTENTS

MY LIFE IN
BRASSTOWN

An Appalachian Memoir

INTRODUCTION

After graduating from Vassar College in 1941, I wanted to see more of the world beyond New York and New England. Ideally, I hoped to teach young adults as a way to see other parts of the country. Teaching opportunities were scarce in the closing years of the Great Depression, and I wrote to schools everywhere in search of work. When I was offered a place on the staff of the John C. Campbell Folk School in Brasstown, North Carolina, I immediately accepted.

I described my year's experience working at the Folk School and becoming part of the Brasstown community in *My Journey to Appalachia*. I wrote that it was Olive Campbell's vision that drew me from New York City to the mountains of North Carolina, "one hundred miles from everywhere." After working with mountain people in Appalachia for several years in the early part of the twentieth century, John and Olive Campbell decided to build a school modeled on the folk schools of Scandinavia. Their plans were delayed by World War I and John's death, but Olive eventually began the task of building a school in memory of her husband. She traveled to Europe with her friend Marguerite Butler to see the Scandinavian folk schools firsthand. Returning to America, they began their search for a suitable location for such a school and found it in Brasstown.

When they inquired at the general store there, the storekeeper, Fred O. Scroggs, welcomed the idea of a school in the community and offered them several acres of land. A meeting of all the people in the community was called, and each family offered materials or labor, and so the building of the school was begun.

Such a school, modeled on Danish schools, was designed for families who hoped to farm the land. The school would teach young people about agriculture and the farm skills needed to raise good livestock and healthy food. Students could learn about carpentry, blacksmithing, and home arts such as meal planning, cooking, sewing, weaving, and health.

The John C. Campbell Folk School was subsequently founded in 1925 to teach these life skills to young adults in the country and to form a cooperative community. The school gave no grades and offered no credit. It was not competitive but was designed to preserve country arts and crafts and to make self-sufficiency possible, as well as to improve the quality of country life. The folk school concept reminded me of programs that had helped farmers during the Great Depression, and so Mrs. Campbell's dream appealed to me as I graduated from college. In September of that year I traveled to Brasstown, where I soon fell in love with the Folk School, farming, and my future husband, Monroe Wilson.

Brasstown itself offered all the charms of a rural community, quite a contrast to any place I had lived previously. It straddled the Cherokee and Clay county lines in the southwestern corner of North Carolina, close to the Georgia border. Murphy, the nearest city of any size, was about eight miles to the west. The Folk School occupied 360 acres in Brasstown and used much of that land to raise crops and graze livestock. In many ways it was a self-sufficient and self-contained community.

At the heart of the Folk School was Keith House. It served as the girls dormitory and housed the kitchen and dining room, as well as classrooms. Here everyone gathered for Morning Song to begin the school day, and the ever-popular Friday Night Games were held in the adjoining Community Room. Various small buildings—a laundry, a museum, an open house for dancing in the warm weather—clustered around Keith House.

It was decided early on that the school would teach folk dancing. To avoid any association with square dancing, which was often accompanied by drinking, the activity was called *games* instead of *dances*. The Folk School's Friday Night Games were a significant social event within the Brasstown community. For many years, the games were taught by Marguerite Butler Bidstrup and her husband, Georg, who also served as the school's farm manager. The Bidstrups lived in half of another dwelling called Mill House; the other half, where a waterwheel pumped water throughout the school property, served as the boys' dormitory.

The first building at the fledgling Folk School was Farm House, where Olive Campbell and Louise Pitman lived. During the winter of my year at the school, I moved to Farm House with Mrs. Campbell while Louise was traveling to arrange sales of crafts to benefit the school. Both women were extraordinary teachers and friends, rich in talent and creativity.

Miss Ruth Gaines was the dietician and chief cook who taught nutrition and cooking to the girls at the school. She was also the girls' dormitory housemother at Keith House. Mr. Leon Deschamps taught the boys surveying and all sorts of small repair tasks, such as replacing window glass, light bulbs, and fence poles. Mr. Deschamps and his wife, Mae, lived in Rock House.

Herman and Mabel Estes and their three daughters occupied a house on the school property. Herman was the woodworking instructor who cut out the rough blocks for the animals that were carved by people in the community and finished in the shop at the school. Murray Martin was hired by Mrs. Campbell to teach both weaving and carving. Items like place mats and carved animals were sold to earn money for the school. My job was to pack and ship orders that the school received from individuals and shops all over the country.

Farming was a completely new experience for me, and I quickly volunteered to feed the chickens and try my hand at milking the cows. A special attraction at the dairy barn was Monroe Wilson, a flirty and funny young man from Georgia. His name was pronounced *Mon*roe, accented in a way I had not heard before. "Muns" and I became fast friends during my year at the Folk School; *My Life in Brasstown* relates our life together and my further appreciation for the people and culture of Appalachia.

Everyone in our family feels that the Folk School is *our* school. We participated in so many of the activities over the years that it was our home away from home, as important a part of the community as the general store at the corner and the Little Brasstown Baptist Church on the hill. Over the years there have been many changes in the Brasstown community. The influence of the Folk School has spread throughout Western North Carolina and beyond. Students now come from all over the world. Many have been charmed by the community and have relocated here.

Though I concluded with a brief epilogue, many people who read *My Journey to Appalachia* have asked what happened after that book ended. This sequel is a more detailed account of our home and community life in the forty years between 1942 and 1982. I chose to end my narrative at that time because my children were grown and seeking lives of their own.

KEEPING IN TOUCH

It was June 1942. Our country had been at war for six months. Anger toward the Japanese was rampant. In our small community of Brasstown, North Carolina, more and more men and boys were volunteering to go to war. All eligible men had registered with the draft board and had received their assigned numbers.

I was deeply in love with Monroe Wilson, a native of north Georgia and a fellow worker at the John C. Campbell Folk School where we met. We talked often about marriage. We were both committed to each other and planned to live in Brasstown, although we were not quite ready to settle down. Monroe had asked me to marry but was reluctant to get married because of his fear that he would not live through the war or would be permanently disabled by it.

I had not been home to Cedarhurst, Long Island, for almost a year, and for most of my teenage years I was away at boarding school and college. I needed the perspective of home to evaluate my life and the traumatic events of our country's involvement in the war.

Going home to New York after so much time in Brasstown would be difficult. I hated to leave the Folk School, Monroe, and the charm of life in the country, but I thought that for the duration of the war I needed to check out home and family. I was optimistic that the war in Europe was coming to a close and that our country would not take long to defeat the Japanese in the Pacific.

After the June Short Course at the Folk School, Mrs. Campbell suggested that Monroe could borrow the school car and drive me to Asheville to catch the train to New York. We talked all the way.

Then on the cinder block platform beside the tracks of the Southern Railway Station in Asheville, self-conscious of other people around us, we embraced and kissed each other good-bye in the polite reticent way of that time. I boarded the passenger car and settled myself by a window, my assorted possessions piled around me. With tears streaming down my cheeks, I waved to Monroe through the clouded window. Although I had heard that in wartime many trains were redirected from areas serving civilian parts of the country to areas where military movement was urgent, my coach was sparsely filled.

The train stopped briefly in Black Mountain and then started down the mountain. It was late afternoon, and we were leaving the sun behind us, sinking lower in the west. I slumped down in my seat, so sad to be leaving my life in the mountains behind me. I munched the roast beef sandwich that Miss Gaines had made for me with Folk School whole wheat bread. What a good friend she had been! It certainly cheered me to relieve my hunger.

As we reached the plateau beyond Old Fort, I relaxed and dozed a bit. Darkness settled over the landscape. Street lamps and the lights in small houses along the tracks cheered the path with evidence of ongoing life. We slowed for the occasional small town and sometimes picked up a passenger.

In Salisbury, North Carolina, in the middle of the night the economy passengers had to dismount and wait for the northbound train to arrive. The Pullman car on our train was switched to a siding to be picked up when the express train from New Orleans came through. So while those passengers slept, we waited sleepily on the platform for the coach that would be coming with the express. I peered through the darkness for the single headlight of the oncoming train.

The company of other lonely figures gathered in small clusters on the dimly lighted platform cheered me, but there was no one who even looked familiar. Soft night breezes filled the air with railroad smells of coal dust and diesel fuel, while nostalgia for the blue mountains and green grass of Brasstown gripped my heart.

When the train finally roared in and came to a screeching stop, trainmen with waving arms swung down from every car. I spotted my coach and clambered up with the help of a kindly conductor who noticed my motley collection of baggage: suitcase, coat, books, camera, snacks, umbrella, and cardboard box of miscellaneous things I hadn't been able to mail home.

The coach was packed with wartime travelers and servicemen, being reassigned to new posts or off on short leaves. There was not an empty seat in the car. A sleepy sailor in a front seat got up to give me his place. I sank gratefully into place. We exchanged stories. He had left his young wife in Fayetteville and was eager to talk a while. Soon, however, sleepiness overtook us both, thanks to the dimmed lights and the regular clickety-clack of the wheels turning on the rails.

I was exhausted, but it was difficult to get more than forty winks. Throughout the night servicemen and most civilians, wedged in every conceivable space in that car, were in a celebratory mood. The trip was a short holiday from their daily responsibilities and merriment was in order. As I joined in, I realized that I was now very different from the serious, naive, idealistic college graduate who had abandoned the Northeast ten months ago in order to see the world. My shy self-conscious self seemed to have dissolved; I now made friends with strangers easily.

Finally the wartime camaraderie of travel calmed. I slept fitfully, lulled by the surf-like sway of the cars as we finally rushed across the swamps of New Jersey, under the Hudson River, and into New York's Pennsylvania Station. Somewhat frazzled, I tumbled out the nearest door and gathered my belongings on the station platform. Other passengers streamed by me, each hurrying to go his own way. The hustle and bustle of the city was overwhelming and the air was stifling; however, my native New Yorker adaptability came to my rescue quickly. Taking a few deep breaths, I regained my sense of place. New York City, where I was born and lived the first five years of my life, has always had a special place in my heart.

I found my way to the Long Island side of the huge station and checked all my things in one of the large metal lockers. With a thankful sigh of relief, I repaired to the rest room to straighten myself. My mouse-brown hair, usually permanently waved, hung limp, long, and lifeless. I did not want to face my mother looking so pitiful; a shampoo and set would surely parry Mother's customary greeting of "Oh Ellie, what have you done to your hair?" Actually I had not done anything to my hair except wash it once a week and cut it myself. I had been gone for almost a year. It did look a bit drab.

After four years at Vassar and an independent year in the mountains of Western North Carolina, it was not really challenging to be returning to my childhood home in Cedarhurst. Although our country was now at war, I felt as though nothing had changed but me. I left the station and walked east along Thirty-fourth Street. As I passed the Empire State Building on my right, I craned my neck to look up at the towering building. I remembered its construction during the years of the Great Depression. My conservative father predicted then that they would never be able to rent all the offices in such a tall building. As I looked at the windows now, it seemed that many rooms were still empty. However, the elevators were doing a brisk business of carrying sightseers to the top. Then I reached Fifth Avenue and crossed to Best's department store on the corner. The beauty parlor was probably still on the fourth floor. A shampoo and set would surely energize me.

My parents were happy to know I was coming home. My older sister, Barbara, and Mother were working at an attractive gift shop in our suburban neighborhood. Father was still commuting to his office on Wall Street in Manhattan, and my younger sister, Louise, was finishing college.

It was good to sleep again in my own curly maple twin bed, to look over my shelves of books, to enjoy spending time with my family. I was unemployed and it was summertime. I cut the grass in the side yard and helped Father set out plants in the small flowerbed. We all enjoyed going to the Lawrence Beach Club and swimming in the surf and in the pool. Sometimes we played Scrabble or canasta, and every evening we had dinner together, a close and happy family, beginning slowly to move on separate paths. I wrote to Monroe almost every day.

During my years away at boarding school, college, and Brasstown, almost all my childhood friends had gone their own ways. I was bored without friends, a sense of purpose, or a job. Soon I was rescued by an invitation to visit Southwest Harbor, Maine, where my college roommate, Liz Foote, and her family had a summer home. It was a beautiful place on a point looking out into the Atlantic Ocean.

Liz's dad was a Unitarian minister, and her mother was a Quaker. They were wonderful, loving people who welcomed Liz's friends every June after college classes were over. Each morning we raced down the lawn to the dock and dived into the ice-cold water. We played tennis and sailed whenever weather and wind cooperated. I felt at home there and loved the whole family. Liz's mother exhibited a really down-to-earth faith in God. I have remembered her kindness and understanding toward all people all my life. That summer visit restored my sense of purpose. I knew I wanted to have a faith like hers and the kindness and understanding toward everyone that she showed so plainly.

Then another former college roommate, Peg Greene, invited me to Cambridge, Massachusetts, where she was living at home while her parents spent the summer months in New Hampshire. It was wonderful to catch up with the news from college roommates and friends. My third roommate, Ann Nash, was married and still living in her hometown of Savannah while her husband was in the service. Liz Foote was in a second year of graduate school in Boston, preparing to be a medical social worker. Peg was finishing her second year studying architecture.

I was homesick for Brasstown and desperately lonely for Monroe. I needed to prepare for some life work more challenging than the clerical task of shipping crafts, which I had done at the Campbell Folk School. I wanted to get a graduate degree in rural sociology or teaching, but I didn't know how to finance it. My parents were helping my sister Louise finish college, and everything I had earned in Brasstown had gone to pay off my college loan.

Later that summer Mother rented a cottage in Pemaquid Point, Maine, for a short vacation. She invited her friend Pauline Urbano and her son Paul to join us for a few days. I was not interested in him, nor he in me! I spent a good bit of time fishing for flounder off the rocks on the breakwater, remembering all the good times when Monroe and I had fished Little Brasstown Creek.

A blackout had been prescribed all along the East Coast of the United States. In Maine, even though our cottage was a few blocks inland, we kept shades pulled at night. There were ration stamps for all the food shortages and especially for meat, so we enjoyed the plentiful fresh fish. On occasion we all went to the Lobster Pound on the wharf where the fishing boats unloaded the catch of the day. There we could each select a dark green live lobster just off the boat for a dollar a pound. The cook dropped them into a huge caldron of steaming water. Then as we watched, he lifted each gleaming red creature onto our plates. Mother usually brought a huge bowl of potato salad and some rolls. We walked out on the pier to wooden picnic tables and enjoyed our feast!

With our guests, we rode bicycles on the shell-paved side roads and enjoyed a bountiful fish fry on the rocks by the lighthouse at noon on Sunday. Father had not been able to join us because of the pressure of work on Wall Street during the war. We missed his company and needed to get back to keep him from being lonely too long. On our last morning before leaving, we breakfasted on the rocks at sunrise before we headed toward home. Barbara and Mother needed to go back to their jobs, but they dropped me in Cambridge to visit Peg again and to look for work.

APPRENTICE TEACHING

❧

Liz and Peg urged me to stay in Cambridge. They recommended Shady Hill School, a wonderful private school there with an excellent teacher-training program. I applied for the course and was accepted for an unpaid position as an apprentice teacher for the sixth grade.

The school gave me a list of families nearby who were looking for "mother's helpers" in exchange for room and board, and I visited several. I quickly came to an agreement with Mrs. Fidelia Taylor, whose situation offered me many advantages. The Taylors' large, white, shingled home was close to Shady Hill; Mrs. Taylor was a Vassar graduate, so we already had much in common; and the children were older than those in most of the families who needed a mother's helper.

The Taylor children were Oliver, in the fifth grade at a private school for boys in Cambridge, and Joan, in the ninth grade at Shady Hill; Mrs. Taylor needed someone to stay with them on weekends or evenings when she was attending meetings, socializing, or visiting her husband in Washington, D.C. Dr. Taylor, a professor on leave from Harvard University, was a colonel in the Naval Reserve. He had volunteered to return to active service for the duration of the war and was stationed at Dumbarton Oaks.

My duties were to help prepare breakfast and dinner, wash dishes, and stay at home on weekends and evenings when Mrs. Taylor had other responsibilities. I had my own room and bath. Quickly I became part of the family. It was Mrs. Taylor who taught me how to cook and keep the kitchen spotless. Casseroles were then a new style of cuisine, and she researched those easy to prepare, did all the shopping, and encouraged me to invite friends for dinner. Both she and Joan were wonderful companions and advisors. I didn't see as much of Oliver, who was a busy, well-behaved eleven year old, occupied with puzzles and building projects as well as his schoolwork.

The walk to school was a short one, just up the hill. Every afternoon when I came home, I found my mail waiting for me on top of the white chest on the porch. More often than not, it included a letter from Monroe in his sprawling scrawl. That became for me the highlight of each day. I could hardly wait to get to my room to read it!

I didn't have a bicycle, but to visit my friends or to shop I had the trolley line into Cambridge and could catch it just at the bottom of the hill. I soon found my way around town and across the Charles River into Boston on occasion. Often I walked along the river, feeling the cold north wind blowing through the thin jacket I had worn comfortably all winter in Brasstown.

I couldn't have made a wiser choice than Shady Hill School in preparing for a teaching career. Every teacher at the school was superb, each aptly suited for the subjects and the ages of the students. The beginners were three year olds, and the graduating class was the ninth, from which students went on to other private schools.

The sixth grade was divided into two sections. Miss Anne Thorpe was the head teacher and I was her apprentice. She focused on teaching English and American history to both sections of the sixth grade. Miss Thorpe had lived American history and literature all her life, as had her many intellectual friends. She was born into a family that dated back to the revolutionary era in Massachusetts. Their historic mansion in the country outside of Boston had been home for generations of Thorpes.

Anne Thorpe was gracious in manner and very kind; her standards were high and she held her students and me to them. She felt a strong responsibility to share the blessings of her life by teaching children all that she had learned about history through community, family, customs, and education. While I was too preoccupied with my absence from the mountains of Western North Carolina and my friends there—especially Monroe—to be able to fully appreciate all that Miss Thorpe taught me, I will always remember her wisdom and kindness.

There were special teachers who moved through the grades from beginners to the ninth grade every day for art, music, athletics, and mathematics. I observed them with interest as they came into the sixth-grade classes. My favorite to watch was the math teacher. She was a woman of short stature, but very tall on enthusiasm. We could hear her approaching, her head full of the number problems that led her on. She bounced into the classroom with questions bombarding the air ahead of her.

"How many panes of glass in the second window?"

"Twelve."

"No."

Hands waved frantically, begging to give the right answer.

"How many?"

"Sixteen?"

"Right!"

"Who is the shortest person in the class?"

"What's the difference between 32 and 10?"

"If we have four rows, with six people in three of them and two in the fourth, how many are in the class?"

Several wild guesses, and then, "Twenty?"

"Right!

So it went in the fun warm-up before she settled down to go over the next lesson carefully in detail. It was almost impossible not to hear the enjoyment she found in problem solving. Even the children who thought they didn't like mathematics became puzzle solvers. She laid the groundwork for algebra so thoroughly that the students went into it almost happily in the seventh grade.

Apprentices observed all the teachers, helped with lesson plans, and corrected papers. Of course, I knew and enjoyed each of the children in our grade, including several especially gifted and talented students. We apprentices had our own classes after school in psychology, child development, and the many methods and history of teaching. We were encouraged to socialize together in our free time, and, of course, we did. It was a good support group.

Even though I didn't know then if I ever wanted to be a classroom teacher, I found many teaching styles at Shady Hill School that I later copied, as best I could. Each teacher thoroughly enjoyed doing wonderful work with interested children, an ideal situation that I would find somewhat difficult to duplicate ever. In 1947 after I returned to North Carolina, all that I had learned in my year at Shady Hill was recognized by the State Teachers Review Board as enough to qualify me for a topnotch teaching certificate in North Carolina, equal to a graduate degree in elementary education.

VISITING MONROE

Monroe and I had exchanged letters almost daily for five months. We determined that Washington was halfway between Brasstown and Cambridge. So, at Shady Hill's Thanksgiving break, I emptied my sock-it-away piggy bank and took the train to Union Station in Washington, D.C. We would meet at the information booth in the station and spend three days together before getting back to work.

On arrival I found, to my surprise, that the information center at Union Station stretched all the way across the station. I walked around and around scanning the crowds with excitement but saw not a sign of Monroe. In desperation I went to the stationmaster and pleaded for help. "Mr. Wilson, please report to gate number one to meet your party there," boomed out over the loud speaker. In relief and joy we were reunited.

"What were you going to do if you couldn't find me, Monroe?"

"Get back on the train and return to Asheville," was his smug reply.

We decided to get out of the city and took a bus to a small town in Virginia. We found a neat little rooming house that appeared respectable and reserved our rooms. We celebrated Thanksgiving by eating dinner in a cheap restaurant, where I remember we ate spinach that was still gritty. Then we walked in a country cemetery and later sat through a movie we didn't even watch. Time flew by until we returned to Union Station. As we parted to go our separate ways, we were surer than ever of the future that lay before us.

Life in Cambridge that winter was good in spite of the distance that separated Monroe and me. I saw old friends and made new ones. I especially enjoyed the company of an apprentice teacher for the fifth grade, Emma Cadbury. She was perceptive and kind and knew that I needed a friend. As a Quaker she invited me to the Friends meeting on several occasions. I had been a pacifist of conviction since my college years, when I had joined an organization called the Fellowship of Reconciliation. It provided mutual support for members, but I had lost contact with other members during my year in the South. Once again I found comfort in a group that shared my ideals about peace. I appreciated having friends with whom to discuss my conflicting sentiments and theology. Everyone else around me seemed to support the war effort and didn't want to question whatever our country was doing, often making conversation difficult.

Sporadically I dated a young artist in the group, Andy Hall, and delivered several of his paintings to galleries in Boston for exhibition. He was limited in his freedom to travel because of his draft status as a conscientious objector.

To supplement my nonexistent income, I took on the task of teaching Sunday school to the first and second graders at the Unitarian church on Harvard Square. A wonderful older lady in whose footsteps I tried to follow was retiring after many years. She knew the children and the Bible and was superbly organized. I couldn't fill those qualifications, but I really needed the weekly pay.

I had no idea what to expect of young children and no concept of appropriate discipline. After two or three Sundays of absolute chaos, I had to admit my first major defeat. Little children were not going to be the recipients of all my wisdom and knowledge. So I resigned my great paying job and walked back home in order to save the ten-cent trolley fare.

I saved pennies again in my sock-it-away bank to travel to Cedarhurst for Christmas at home with my family. Thankfully, I collected some much needed Christmas gift checks. When I returned to Cambridge I managed to land a few baby-sitting jobs.

Monroe wrote that his draft number was getting close to the drawing point and he would have to volunteer for the navy soon or be drafted into the army. He did not like the prospect of having to fight on the ground in the dirt of the trenches. I did not even believe in the drafting of people into the service, but I knew he was doing what he believed was right, and he certainly wasn't willing to discuss it. Although I often felt uncomfortable with patriotic enthusiasm for war, I respected loyalty and responsibility.

As spring vacation approached, Monroe and I again made plans to meet. I wrote to Mrs. Campbell to tell her that I would like to visit the Folk School and soon received an invitation to stay at Keith House. I bought a ticket on the Greyhound bus from Cambridge to Murphy, packed a suitcase and a bag of snacks, and set out for North Carolina. It was a wonderful way to see bus stations in cities and small towns all down the East Coast, but agonizingly slow!

Monroe was still in charge of the Folk School dairy herd. He had the use of the school truck, met me in Murphy at the bus station, and took me to Keith House. That week we visited several married couples in Brasstown, exchanging news of the past year, and enjoying the thought that we might soon be able to join their group in Brasstown. In the midst of our visit with Jewell Rogers and her newborn son, Paul, we were called back to Keith House. Marguerite Bidstrup, looking very serious, met us at the door. Kindly, she inquired, "Was your father ill when you left to come down here?"

"No, Marguerite, he was fine." I replied, feeling uneasy. Then she told me he had died earlier that morning. I was speechless. I felt numb. It was the first of April. Father had always loved to tease Mother with mild tricks on April Fool's Day. As children we had enjoyed the fun, but Mother always said she hated that day. My sister Barbara discovered Father on the morning of April 1, 1943, sitting in his armchair in the living room. After tending the furnace in the cellar, he had stopped to rest and have a cigarette. He died instantly of a cerebral hemorrhage at the age of sixty-six, his unsmoked cigarette smoldering slowly beside his chair.

My mother wanted me to come home at once. The Folk School offered the school car and enough of their wartime gas ration for Monroe to drive me to Asheville where I could catch the train back to New York. The long, lonely night gave me time to grieve by myself. Father had always been a special friend to me, as well as a good father.

I was devastated and ill prepared for this unexpected turn of my life. It is so easy to take the good everyday events of life for granted. However, I did not question God or rail at the unfairness of my father's death. With grateful thanks for the time I had had with him, I remembered him.

At home as a child, I always sat at the dinner table halfway between my mother and my father, dividing my attention equally. Mother was fun and critical; Father was quiet and interesting. He talked with me about politics and life and people he had loved and lost, remembering funny stories about his childhood and Sam, his Irish setter.

I knew he loved and respected me and thought of me often. He sent me fruit cakes from the Savarin restaurant regularly while I was in college. I remembered the special days when he took me to dinner at a wonderful hotel uptown in New York when I was home on vacation or when he told me I was pretty when I came down from college to go with him to Auntie's funeral.

On vacations on Nantucket Island each summer, he woke me early in the morning at least once during his short vacation with us there. Noticing the wildflowers and listening to the bird songs, we walked together through the country before the rest of the family was up and ready for breakfast.

I loved my father dearly, understood his quick temper that exploded on occasion, and often distracted his mind by asking him questions about his work as a stockbroker or his Republican politics. I was numb and unbelieving in grief, but tearless. He would want me to be brave.

All was confusion and sorrow at home. I found it very difficult and was given no role in the funeral ceremony at church. Mother insisted that we wear mourning bands on our left arms, and I felt conspicuous and a little odd. After the funeral I went back to Cambridge, finished my year at Shady Hill, and returned home to live with my mother and sister in Cedarhurst for the next two years.

Waiting Time

I had no definite plans for that summer after my father died. My visit to Brasstown in the spring had been curtailed, and I wanted to see Monroe once more before he might be called into service. I wrote to Louise Pitman to ask if they had work for me at the Folk School, and she replied to say that they would give me a scholarship to the June Short Course if I would stay into July and help with the farm work at the school. Brasstown men had almost all been taken into service, and the school needed help with the bumper crop of wheat that year. Monroe, too, was no longer at the Folk School. Rather than being drafted into the army, he had enlisted in the navy. He went home to stay with his mother until being called to training in the navy.

I went back to my own little room in Farm House. When the threshing machine drew up to the entrance of the big barn in which the wheat had been stored, I helped from daylight to dark. It was a wonderful, noisy, dusty new experience for me and more exciting than my daily routine helping with the milking in the barn. Moreover, I loved this taste of farm life; it was better than any of the team sports I had enjoyed all my life.

Monroe borrowed his cousin's car and came up to see me several times. Again we discussed our future together. His uncertainty about his fate made him reluctant to set any date for marriage, but he earnestly persuaded me of his sincerity. This was not unusual. Many young couples were waiting for the war to be over before stepping into marriage. Others were marrying hurriedly and regretting the long separation as the husband went overseas to live or die.

One day Monroe picked me up and took me to see where he grew up and to meet his family. It was a winding drive down to Hemp, Georgia. Monroe pointed out the difference in the pavement as we left the macadam roads of North Carolina and crossed into Georgia, where taxes did not cover road maintenance. Mending potholes and keeping the highways' edges sharp had to depend on the voluntary work of the people who lived along the road. When we crossed the line into Fannin County, where he had been born and lived all his life, Monroe cheered—facetiously. He rounded another curve or two and turned off the paved road onto a dirt road between two fields of waist-high corn. We bumped over a high plank bridge that crossed well above a small branch.

"That's where I used to set my traps on the way to school in the morning," he told me. "Then when I came home, I released the ones I didn't want and skinned the mink or beaver or otter. Those were skins I could send off for sale." We kept going and stayed to the right when we came to a fork in the rutted road, climbing into a yard directly in front of the house. A few steps there led up to an open porch. "Jerry will be here, too," Monroe said, by way of preparation. He took my arm up the steps and opened the front door without further formality. Jerry and Mama Wilson were sitting on the couch as we came in. Both jumped up and hugged us both warmly!

It was a great visit. They were welcoming and kind, offering me something to eat and inquiring about my mother and how she was doing after the death of my father. Before Monroe's sister Jerry was married, I had met her briefly at the Folk School. Her husband, Hoyt Thomas, was in the army, and she was staying with her mother. We exchanged news of ourselves happily, off to a good start. Later that afternoon, Monroe and I drove up to Vogel Lake for a swim and then Monroe took me back to the Folk School, where I stayed for a few more days before returning to Long Island to look for a job.

The Pennsylvania Railroad was recruiting clerks to replace men and women who were leaving to join the army. Friends told me it was good work, paying railroad retirement if you stayed in for life. I applied for my Social Security number and began working as a clerk in the information booth on the Long Island side of the terminal.

I knew the commuter system well. Our childhood lifestyle involved not only my father's daily commute, but also our regular shopping trips into New York City for clothes, entertainment, museums, and visits with Auntie, the grandmother figure in my life. I had even commuted regularly to the New York Public Library during Christmas vacation at college in 1940 to do research for a senior paper on the rise of the advertising industry.

The information booth was an open, multisided affair situated where various traffic patterns crossed in the busiest part of the station. Everyone was in a hurry, running for his or her connection, asking for the right track at the last minute. Many had taken time to grab a snack and a newspaper before seeking information. Several clerks manned the booth, rotating positions to consult different schedules on the timetables under glass between the counters. I loved the job, helping people of all shapes and sizes, all kinds of manners and forms of speech and foreign accents. Everyone needed information and directions, and I was there to supply them quickly.

Once in a while, out of the melee, a familiar figure appeared, and we had a mini reunion. No one complained when we took the time to visit briefly. Even a few people whom I had known in Brasstown chanced to come by, and we rejoiced in our mutual "small world."

However, soon I was transferred to the ticket counter to sell tickets to the racetrack at Belmont Park, a completely different experience. There I learned always to watch my change. The ticket cost some odd amount like eighty-two cents. Everyone was in a hurry to catch the train and not miss the race on which they were betting. They slapped down a dollar and grabbed the ticket and the eighteen cents change, but sometimes only seventeen cents. Or they plunked down some change that required a quick eye: five dimes, a quarter, a nickel and a few pennies. We started the day with a fixed amount of change and at the close of our day were required to return that amount plus all that we had made in our sales. Needless to say, we were careful, but it was easy to short-change a quick customer by a nickel or a penny or two.

My post lasted only as long as the season of scheduled races at Belmont Park. Then I was transferred to telephone information upstairs, out of the rushing crowds. It was an evening job. I found it ideal for the summer. I was alone at home while Mother and Barbara were on vacation on Nantucket. I slept late. Then I rode my bicycle over to the inlet where friends had a dock, and took a quick swim. Then I went home for a sandwich and left enough time to ride to the railway station, padlock the bike to the iron gate there, and take the train in for an evening's work.

Again I was looking at timetables and schedules and helping people manage time and place. I loved finding the way from city to city across the country, exploring alternate routes. I liked working in the cool of the evening, finishing around midnight. Then after work, I loved stopping at the Savarin in the Long Island Railroad Station for a cheese sandwich and a cold beer before boarding the train for Cedarhurst where I unchained my bicycle and rode home through the deserted suburban streets in the cool of night.

I thoroughly enjoyed the independence until Mother and Barbara returned from vacation. They were horrified at the danger they imagined for me riding home in the night. Mother insisted that I resign and stay at home, and so I did. I suppose it was good to have a break before school started anyway. I had been hired as the junior high social studies teacher at Friends Seminary on Nineteenth Street in New York. I could stay at home and contribute to household expenses. With Father gone, Mother was stretching the budget to see that Louise could finish her senior year at Vassar.

Monroe was now in training at the navy boot camp in Maryland. He was able to come to New York to visit with our friend Philip Merrill, who had played the piano and fiddle regularly for June Short Courses and Christmas parties at the Folk School; then Monroe came out to Cedarhurst to spend the weekend and meet my mother and sister.

Mother loved to hear him talk. She immediately appreciated his humor. When she asked if he was afraid of drowning if the ship sank, he laughed and told her he thought he could tell enough jokes to keep the sharks from eating him. Mother found it impossible not to like Monroe. After that visit, he was off to Detroit to learn to be an engineer through the V-12 Navy College Training Program.

TEACHING AT FRIENDS SEMINARY

For me, it was time to begin my teaching career. Every morning I caught the Long Island train into Penn Station and took the subway down to Union Square. Then I walked across Nineteenth Street to school. Sometimes there were men sleeping in doorways as I passed, but usually there were few people walking across town that early in the morning.

Friends, as the seminary was known, was a prestigious private school that was founded by Quakers in 1786. My classroom windows looked out at Stuyvesant Square, a small park. I had a wonderful seventh-grade group of gifted boys and girls. I loved teaching American history to the eighth grade and civics lessons to the seventh. The children were eager to discuss the material and to offer opinions learned from their parents at home or from the media reports. The war was speeding up now that we were moving into the Pacific to fight the Japanese. The geography of the Pacific Islands and the Japanese possessions there was new to me as well as to the students. Learning about it was interesting and important in understanding why we were at war there and what strategy could be used to regain control of our bases.

In many ways my first year at Friends went well, but I often felt a bit isolated. All the teachers were older than I, and they were all more experienced teachers. When I encountered teaching problems or had questions about a student, I had few colleagues with whom I could confer. Generally, they had no close family or friends involved in the war, but I was lonely for Monroe and concerned about his future as he moved into the officers training program. Letters didn't come as often as they had before because he became busy with his classes.

I was fortunate to have my college roommate Liz Foote (now Liz McKay) living in Greenwich Village, not far across town from the school. Liz had a small walk-up apartment on West Eighth Street while Jim, her husband, was stationed in north Africa. I could walk over there after school easily, and usually went late on Thursday afternoons to spend the night with her.

Often I detoured down to East Tenth Street and across to the Village that way. I liked to remember my early childhood. Until I was five years old, our family lived in an apartment at 18 East Tenth Street. Walking that way brought back memories of afternoon outings with our Swedish nurse, Elsa. We often went to a churchyard on Fifth Avenue. I clearly remembered that one day when I was very small, I slipped away by myself to gather pebbles to put in my coat pocket. Much to my disappointment Elsa made me put them back. I had only wanted something to take home to remember the churchyard.

I spent many Thursday nights with Liz, and she came out to Cedarhurst for an occasional weekend. It was a relief for both of us to have someone to share our loneliness and worries. Other evenings I sometimes joined college friends at the English-Speaking Union, where parties were given regularly for English naval officers or others on leave far from home. It was pleasant to dance and befriend an often lonely soul.

I was glad when summer vacation rolled around, and I could return to life at home. There was plenty to do there. In our small backyard, I planted a Victory Garden. There was strict rationing, and the supply of fresh vegetables helped as much as the satisfaction of seeing things grow. In August Mother again rented a small vacation cottage for the month; this year it was "At Last" on Nantucket Island.

Monroe was now finishing the V-12 training in engineering at George Williams College, a part of the University of Chicago. I had promised to visit Monroe sometime during the summer and meant to leave from Boston after my week's vacation on Nantucket. However, an interesting weather pattern emerged on Thursday. I was on the beach in Sconset when warnings of a hurricane were relayed to me. I was able to leave the island on the last steamer before the storm struck, although Mother and Barbara prepared to ride out the storm in their cottage on the island.

The steamer was filled with vacationers trying to get home before the storm stranded them on the island. As we sailed toward Cape Cod, the normally turbulent Atlantic Ocean was as flat as a still pond with "the calm before the storm." Not a wave or even a ripple in the water could be seen, but what would be remembered as the Great Atlantic Hurricane of 1944 was about to hit. At Woods Hole, the train to Boston was packed from door to door with coastal refugees. We arrived in Boston's South Station to find it completely filled with weary people sitting on their luggage as they waited for transportation out.

I located the Travelers' Aid Station where I managed to call, without success, every friend I could remember in the Boston area. The kind officer at the aid station finally told me of a rooming house with a vacancy for one in a third floor walkup. Relieved, I managed to find it. I shampooed and rolled my hair in curlers and slept an hour or two before catching the coach train to Chicago in the morning.

Monroe met me and took me to the YWCA Hostel for Women, where we made my reservation for a week's stay. Accommodations at the typical hostel consisted of large rooms divided into small areas by high wire fences, each with locks on the door and containing only a narrow cot. When I checked in, I was given a key to my enclosure and shown the common locker room with toilets, wash basins, and showers. Hostels provided a very inexpensive way to stay in cities during the 1930s and '40s. They were somewhat similar in informality and expense to the European hostels where traveling college students often stayed.

Monroe showed me all around the campus at the University of Chicago and George Williams College, and then we went out for dinner and a movie. He had to be back in his dormitory at George Williams before the midnight curfew that Friday, but he had wrangled a weekend off and had reserved a small hotel room for himself. Monroe headed back to beat the curfew, but I stayed there that first night. Feeling very adventurous after he left, I opened the Murphy bed that was folded up in the wall. A bit nervous at the thought it might fold back with me asleep, I was glad to know I would have my own place for the balance of my stay. I slept peacefully until he called in the morning, and we went out for breakfast.

We spent the whole weekend exploring Chicago: bus lines, museums, the public library, parks, and the lake; but mostly we talked. Monroe's professors were often refugees from Europe with assorted foreign accents, and he had considerable difficulty with the strongly accented language they used to explain crucial mathematic texts. He was having an especially difficult time understanding the German refugee professor who was teaching advanced calculus. Monroe had been valedictorian of his small high school in Georgia, but they had never offered a class in calculus. He was discouraged and afraid he would fail, or that the navy would close the V-12 program and he would have no further classes in college. It was a relief for him to be able to talk about it, but he moved quickly to funny stories of his adventures in this military world, so different from his life in the mountains!

Particularly he enjoyed sharing stories about his months in Detroit. He had made good friends there—men who liked to take him to their homes on weekends to meet their mothers and sisters. He had even learned to enjoy the foreign foods of some of Detroit's first-generation families. Chicago didn't seem quite as hospitable, perhaps because he was in the university setting instead of with blue-collar engineering co-workers in Detroit. Our weekend ended too soon, not anything like long enough for us. Monroe would have time off on Wednesday afternoon and evening, and we planned to celebrate with dinner and a movie.

Monday morning I set out to explore Chicago alone. I headed to the Field Museum and spent most of the day there, enjoying myself thoroughly. After a late lunch at a drugstore counter on Tuesday, I found the closest bus line. The afternoon was gray and cold. I stayed on the bus from one end of the line to the other; getting back to my lodgings just in time to find a small café, eat supper, and read myself to sleep.

On Wednesday Monroe had the day off and came to check me out of my hostel before another day of sightseeing and an afternoon movie. Then he put me on the train back to New York while he went back to school. The trip to Chicago was a success, all in all, in spite of my having to spend so much time alone. I enjoyed the opportunity to see the city and the lake for myself, but I was ready to get back to New York for my second year at Friends Seminary.

There was a new group of students in the seventh grade and my former class in the eighth. It was a more difficult year for me as my anxiety about Monroe in service increased. The V-12 program was terminated and he was transferred: first to the Great Lakes Training Center, then to San Francisco, and finally to San Diego where his ship, the light cruiser *Tucson*, was commissioned. After that, mail from Monroe came infrequently and in batches. Except for the brief time his ship spent in Pearl Harbor, where he had some time ashore, I never knew exactly where he was until he had moved on. I found it difficult to talk about him without tearing up. However, after Germany surrendered in May 1945, it seemed as if the war would be coming to an end. I was walking to Liz's apartment the afternoon that President Franklin Roosevelt died at Hot Springs. We didn't know much about the vice president, Harry Truman, and wondered to each other about how he would manage the presidency and the end of the war.

I decided not to plan on teaching another year. Instead, I asked the vocational director at Vassar for a list of temporary opportunities. She gave me an address in Rockefeller Center. I went in late one afternoon to interview without knowing exactly what I would be doing. I was accepted and told to report for work early Monday morning, still ignorant as to the nature of this job.

Following directions to the office, I found myself high in the sky at the Rockefeller Foundation. I really had very little idea of what the foundation did, but I soon discovered that it was very busy allocating grant money to projects and institutions all over the country. The reference department to which I was assigned read all the incoming mail and routed it to the proper department chair for consideration of its merit for a grant. I was assigned to the medical and scientific division and read with interest all the requests for grants to those projects. Then I passed them on to each department head for evaluation of appropriate funding.

Much of the work was war related and therefore confidential. However, by putting together bits and pieces as I read, I managed to get glimpses of several experiments related to the development of the atomic bomb in Chicago and some idea of what was happening in Oak Ridge, Tennessee. It was an exciting time to be working. Here was also a friendly group of workers. Most of the readers were in my age bracket, so we often went out for lunch together. I learned to enjoy Chinese food that summer.

Our office windows faced Fifth Avenue with a clear bird's-eye view between the high buildings. The war in Europe ended in May and by midsummer, troops were coming home. Parades were the order of the day. We certainly had front-row places from which to watch as the military victories in north Africa, Italy, and eventually all of Europe were celebrated.

However, news from the Pacific was sparse until the atomic bombs were dropped in August and the war came to an end. All I can remember feeling about those devastating pictures in the papers and newsreels is horror! The rationalizations about this means of bringing the war with Japan to a close brought a mixture of sadness and desperate relief to many, along with great despair over what little regard there was for human life. My solace was that Monroe would finally come home.

And so he would . . . after his ship accompanied a large part of the Pacific Fleet into Tokyo Harbor to witness the signing of the peace treaty. Monroe was able to get a short shore leave in Tokyo and to bring home a souvenir doll's china cabinet from Japan to prove it.

In October 1945, he called from San Diego to say that he had a two-week leave before his ship would be decommissioned and he could come home! He would take the train to New York; could I meet him at the station there? It would be a troop train and would probably take three days to cross the country. It would be Saturday before we would see each other, but he wanted to get married right away. What joy to think that at last we would! I was so excited I told everyone, calling and asking them to celebrate with us. Mother and I began planning a home wedding. I decided that I would like Mr. Foote, Liz McKay's father, to marry us. He was the Unitarian minister I had known so well beginning with the my years in college when I had visited with Liz's family.

Mother called Aunt Lucy in New York and asked her to order the wedding cake. Though not actually my aunt, Lucy was my maternal grandmother's first cousin who had always been an intermittent fairy godmother to my sisters and me. Barbara would be my maid of honor and Philip Merrill would be Monroe's best man. Mother reserved the cottage on Nantucket, "At Last," for our honeymoon.

On Saturday I met Monroe as he arrived, natty in his sailor's uniform! Before we took the train out to Cedarhurst, we found a nice restaurant with a quiet table where we could look at each other and talk. He looked pretty much the same as he had always looked to me, his big green-brown eyes dancing with mischief, then smiling quietly and seriously. I probably talked more and faster than he did, telling him all the plans we had made. For a wedding trip he had thought of going to Atlantic City or Niagara Falls, but I preferred Nantucket and was certain that he would enjoy it.

I told him I just needed a plain gold ring, and he pulled an ivory colored box from his pocket to give me the diamond engagement ring with a matching wedding ring he had bought in Pearl Harbor on his way across the Pacific. I teased that he had won the rings in a poker game, but I was pleased that he had remembered to get the rings before his ship carried him into battle. In living proof of our longtime plan to marry, he had made provision for the wedding and carried the rings with him all the way to Japan. There was much teasing, laughter, and crying. We were pleased with ourselves and with each other. Our deep love had survived the war and the long separation.

We had seen each other's childhood homes and kept in close touch through more than three years of separation. We gained much experience in those wartime years that would serve us well in the future. We both felt ready for marriage, and we were happy that both our mothers approved the match!

The next week was a whirlwind of preparation before actually tying the knot. There were many details of the wedding to be put in place. We needed to ready the house and contact nearby guests. Barbara practiced the wedding march on the piano in the living room. Aunt Lucy promised to bring the cake and some kitchen help on the big day. Barbara would wear the dress she had worn at Louise's wedding to Keith Eaton in Lake Charles, Louisiana, the previous February, and I would wear Louise's wedding dress, which Mother had stored for her. Unfortunately, at this time Louise and Keith felt that they couldn't make the trip to New York for our wedding.

After securing the necessary license, Monroe and I had to appear before a judge to have the waiting period waived. We had waited long enough! Many couples had married in similar hurried circumstances and we found time restraints relaxed and officials understanding. The judge who waived the mandatory waiting period was kind and wished us much happiness.

Then October 18, 1945, arrived. Mr. Foote and Liz came early in the morning. In the back bedroom upstairs, the gentle, kind minister quietly rehearsed Monroe through the brave steps he was taking. Meanwhile, I packed to go on our honeymoon. Aunt Lucy came with the promised help and a huge, magnificent wedding cake. It stood proudly on the dining room table surrounded by Mother's best plates, punch cups, and napkins. At last it was time for the wedding.

The wedding march sounded on the piano, and I came down the hall stairs and swept into the living room. Monroe and Philip were standing in front of the fireplace beside the leather-covered bench in the corner. Mr. Foote stood in the middle, and Mother and Barbara were came to the other side. They say I raced across the living room and looked up at Monroe triumphantly!

The reception was really a party, marred only slightly by the fact that, unbeknownst to Aunt Lucy, the cake had been a display item in the New York bakery window. The thick icing was so stale and hard that we used a hammer instead of a knife to break it into pieces so we could have a bite of the cake inside! Even though Aunt Lucy was embarrassed and we were disappointed, there were hearty bursts of laughter and extra sips of champagne to toast us into happiness, and a second cake was brought from the kitchen for the guests.

Then it was time for us to catch our train and be on our way. Barbara drove us to the train station. I hugged her good-bye fondly and wished her the same degree of happiness soon.

After a wonderful week on Nantucket, it was time to step out of the magic and get ready for life. Monroe went back to San Diego to be discharged after participating in the decommissioning of his ship. He mustered out of the navy as a Seaman First Class and became a civilian veteran to my relief and joy. These formalities took most of a month.

I resigned my place at the Rockefeller Foundation, watched a few more victory parades on Fifth Avenue, and went back to Cedarhurst to pack up wedding presents. Barbara sold me her old 1935 Ford sedan for sixty dollars.

We spent most of December with Mother in Cedarhurst. Early in the month I introduced Monroe to the New York City subway system. Then we went to a big sale at Macy's department store to buy some civilian shirts for him. There I lost him in the crowd—I had to have him paged to meet me at the door! On New Year's Eve we went to Times Square to participate in the Ball Drop at midnight. The crowd again swallowed us up, but we both survived.

We had explored New York and felt comfortable at home in Cedarhurst with Mother and Barbara, but we were restless to see the mountains and Monroe's family. With the coming of the new year we finally felt it was time to pack our car with my clothes, our wedding presents, and Monroe's sea bag; bid a tearful farewell to Mother and Barbara; and chug off to the mountains in our own little Ford we named Rosie.

BACK TO GEORGIA

On January 2, 1946, Monroe and I began our journey south. I was sad at the thought of leaving my childhood home but was really excited too. I held a road map of the eastern part of the United States, and Monroe took the steering wheel. We had no written directions to the Triborough Bridge and New York City, but fortunately I could navigate from memory as far as New Jersey. There we were confronted with many route choices. There were few state highways that joined each other, although rumor had it that there would be interstate highways in the future. The maze of roads through or around each small city and town in New Jersey required navigational skills that we both had acquired one way or another during the war years. We talked our way through New Jersey and on across Pennsylvania, making occasional rest stops and munching the picnic lunches Mother had supplied.

The Shenandoah Valley of Virginia offered no hazards. It was smooth sailing along the new highway there, where blue mountains hugged both sides of the route. Weariness came with dusk as we pushed on through the steeper mountains of southern Virginia. As we left the small town of Wytheville, Rosie refused to climb the curving mountain road. Skillfully Monroe backed down to a rooming house we had passed as we left town. When we went in and asked if they had a room, the owner demanded verification that we were married. We had inadvertently left our marriage license at Mother's, so our word hung in the balance. How could we prove our legal status as husband and wife? This was certainly a new experience for me; how could they possibly doubt my innocence? Thankfully our naive, big-eyed surprise at their question won them over. They had a room *and* the sheets were clean!

The next morning we left early. Monroe managed to get the car up the steep mountain road and over into North Carolina. It was great to see familiar countryside. We both relaxed and enjoyed ourselves. As we drove, Monroe talked about his brothers and sisters, some of whom I would soon be meeting for the first time. He gave me an update on everyone.

Several in the family who were in the service during the war had yet to be discharged, and others were getting ready to go. Mama Wilson was worried that her youngest son, Jarrell, who was with her at home throughout most of the war years, would have to go into the army, probably to be stationed in California. Another son, Olin, was still in the service. Daughter Jerry was waiting for her husband, Hoyt, to be discharged from the army. They lived in Copperhill, Tennessee, not too far away, and would come up to see us as soon as they could. Monroe's sister, Callie, and her husband, Roy McGee, also lived in the Copperhill area. Hoyt and Roy both worked for the Tennessee Copper Company. Our homecoming would be the occasion for much of the family to get together. Mama Wilson, like a brooding hen, enjoyed gathering all her chicks who lived within driving distance, and they all enjoyed visiting each other.

Toward the end of the day we finally reached Georgia. I was dozing lightly when we crossed into Fannin County."We're almost to Hemptown!" Monroe exclaimed, using his nickname for the tiny community he had lived in most of his life. His jubilant shout woke me, filling my heart with awareness of his deep longing for home. For the next few miles he slowed around the curves in the narrow asphalt highway as he recognized familiar homes and neighbors. Then we left the road and bounced on the narrow rutted drive across farm fields and up to the gray weather-beaten house on the slope of a hill. The wide porch stretched welcoming arms as Mama Wilson swung open the front door and came out to watch our progress as we neared the yard. Then, in her simple dress covered with a freshly starched apron ready to catch her tears of joy, she came down quickly to meet us.

Monroe barely pulled to a full stop in the yard before he was in his mother's bear hug. I followed and she hugged me tightly too. "I kept supper for you," she said. Then she led us through the front room into the kitchen. The dining table was set with two places marked by glasses of milk. There were serving bowls of mashed potatoes, soup beans, and applesauce; and platters of sliced ham and cornbread. We persuaded her to sit with us while we ate. There was no need for her to stand by waiting to refill the plates—we were starved, and it all tasted like home.

After supper she took us into the front room where the big feather bed was made up. It was topped with the countless quilts she had made for us as wedding presents. There was an improvised closet of hooks and nails in the wall behind the door in one corner. A chamber pot sat conveniently on the floor at the bottom of the bed.

Mama Wilson said it was always best after a meal to let the dishes rest a while. That gave us time to unpack the car. While I took charge of hanging up our clothes, Monroe stepped out the front door of our room onto the porch and was gone for a few minutes. I greeted his return with "Where did you go, Muns?"

"Bad news," he said. "I thought I was going to the outhouse, but it isn't there. There's just a pile of boards where it used to be. I built a new one just before I left for the navy, and I thought it would still be here. I've been gone longer than I thought. We'll just have to use the bushes. I'll show you the trail up the hill back of the house." So much for my introduction to country living! It was a huge step for me considering the modest Victorian upbringing I had received from my mother.

Mama slipped out to do the dishes and her evening chores. There was a well on the side porch with a windlass to bring up a bucket of water. Each evening she drew up two buckets of "night water" to set in the kitchen ready for cooking breakfast.

We stayed with Mama Wilson for all of January. Monroe kept busy making improvements for his mother. First he dug a deep pit for an outhouse. Over it he built a rough four-sided shelter with a wide two-hole bench inside. It had a tin roof and a door that hooked shut from the inside. The next day he went to town and bought an electric pump to put in the well so that his mother wouldn't have to draw up water by hand.

I helped as best I could in the kitchen. Mama Wilson taught me how to make biscuits the way she had made them all her life. Her long oval-shaped wooden dough tray was on the counter next to the wood stove where she cooked. It was always full of flour with a dish towel draped over it. When she was ready to bake biscuits, she rounded out a hole in the center of the flour and poured in about a cup of milk, a pinch of salt, some baking soda, and a good-sized dollop of melted lard. She stirred that into a ball of dough, then rolled it between both hands into a thick rope. She pinched off generous round biscuits and placed them side by side in a huge baking pan. When she let me try, we both laughed as I twisted dough back and forth, entwining it between my fingers where it refused to let go. She helped me extricate myself from the process and scraped it all back into the bowl.

"Never mind," she said cheerfully. "It takes practice. Just keep trying. I wager that the biscuits I've made in my lifetime would stretch from here to California if they were lined up straight," she bragged. "You'll get better."

The morning after we arrived at Mama Wilson's, Monroe pointed out the nearest neighbors. His brother Bill lived on the highway across from the rutted road leading to the homeplace with his wife, Elvela, and their two children, four-year-old Larry and his baby sister, Angie.

Off to the right of Mama Wilson's house, and just out of sight around a gentle hill, was the dairy farm of Monroe's youngest sister, Maggie, and her husband, Lewin Brackett. They lived in the house that originally belonged to Monroe's grandparents. John Herman and Magdalene Wilson built on this land-grant property back in the mid-1800s as the first Wilson couple to settle in the area. Now Maggie and Lewin and their two small children, Bobby and Sandy, lived there and farmed the land.

As Monroe was giving me a bird's-eye tour of the neighborhood, we had our first company. Two young blond-headed boys appeared at the edge of the yard near the front of our car. "Is Uncle *Mon*roe here?" shouted the two in unison before coming closer. Monroe walked down and after a friendly tussle came back with the two small cousins, his nephews. Bobby was on his shoulders and Larry was clutching his hand.

It was a warm January day and we sat in the straight chairs on the long front porch. Soon Maggie appeared. She told us that last night when they all saw our car parked at Grandma's house they guessed that Uncle Monroe had come home from the war. Larry begged his mother to let him go up to see him. So early that morning he came across the field from his house on the highway to get Bobby to go with him up to Grandma's.

Neither of the little boys really knew their Uncle Monroe because they were so small when he left for the navy, but they had listened to the family worry about him and pray for him for four years, and they wanted to see him. Larry was shy enough to need Bobby's company to go with him. Maggie then followed the boys to make sure they were both safe. The young boys essentially had free run of nearly one hundred acres, but all the family kept an eye out for them.

After we had been home for about a week, Monroe decided to take a break from work around the house and introduce me to his oldest sister. "Myrtle is really my other mother," he explained. "She was twenty when Jarrell was born. While Mother was taking care of the baby boys, Jarrell and Olin, Myrtle took care of all of us who were half grown. Myrtle is married to Lorraine Murrell, and they live in Lenoir City, near Knoxville."

So we set off on another adventure, driving north through the Tennessee River Valley. It was warm and almost springlike with redbud trees along the roadsides beginning to show promise in the mauve outlines of their thin branches. We saw many well-tended small farms in the rolling hills as we neared Lenoir City. We soon found the tiny trailer Myrtle and Lorraine had set up in the corner of a friend's field. Myrtle was heavy set, dark haired, and very congenial. She was so pleased to see us that she positively twittered with excitement. They had moved close to Knoxville when Lorraine had work with the Tennessee Valley Authority, but now that work was completed and he was doing odd jobs for people in the community.

He took time off to welcome us. Their only daughter, Ada, had finished high school and moved to a job in Georgia.

Myrtle was homesick for all her family so they rolled out the red carpet for us. I thought Monroe would never get to the end of his stories about the navy and all he had seen of the world. They could not get enough of him! After three nights there it started raining. That certainly put a damper on our sightseeing in Knoxville, so we thanked them for a good visit and left for home.

Back in Hemp we tried to visit as much more of the family as possible. Bessie was Monroe's second oldest sister and perhaps closest to him in personality. After church on Sunday, she and her husband, Jewel Sparks, their sons, Kenneth and Lamar, and six-month-old daughter, Erma, came to Mama Wilson's for dinner. Bessie urged us to visit their house while we were home. She said that she and Erma were usually alone most of the day while the boys were in school and Jewel was at work.

Bessie had married into the Sparks family, whose history and customs were very similar to those of the Wilson clan. The little house Bessie and Jewel were living in was not far from the homeplace where Mama Wilson grew up and where her mother, Maggie Mashburn, was still living. Jewel worked long hours in his small country store over on the highway. He and Bessie had some cropland and farmed in the summer, cutting hay and putting in a huge garden.

The Sparks' place was at the head of a cove and access by road was not good. As Monroe had already told me, country roads in Georgia at that time were not state maintained. It was up to the people who used them to keep them in good repair, and that was difficult, especially in the winter. So one bright morning we walked over the hill and across fields to Bessie's house. It was a beautiful walk, mostly out of sight of other houses or of any road. The hills were rolling, not difficult to climb, but, as Monroe said, "It's quite a piece." I certainly needed the exercise but managed to keep up with his long strides.

We found Bessie and Erma together in the bedroom when we arrived. Bessie was trying to toilet train the baby so she wouldn't have to wash diapers. She was waving Erma gently over a rubber sheet spread across the bed. We did not get to see how successful she might be because, when we arrived, she stopped the training and dressed Erma. The boys would not be back from school until late afternoon. Often they stayed to walk back with their dad when he closed up the store. Bessie told us she was hoping we'd settle somewhere in the Hemp community and be their neighbors, but Monroe had no intention of living that close to all the family.

Two other siblings, sister Anna Mae and brother Bill, lived nearby. They both worked in Blue Ridge, Georgia, at a hosiery mill and rode together to work. One Saturday we drove over to see Anna Mae and her husband, Perry Bruce. Anna Mae was short in stature and plump. She fastened her long brown hair in a bun at the back of her neck and moved quickly. She was very good at explaining how she and Perry managed the farm. They lived in a sturdy, old, log barn that had seen many years there on the place.

Anna Mae and Perry had converted the barn into a temporary home while they saved enough money to build their dream house on the property. The dwelling spoke loudly of the ingenuity of the Bruces. They certainly knew how to improvise and manage. At one end of the barn a big stone fireplace had been built, and a curtain created a bedroom at the other end.

Anna Mae cooked in the fireplace. She showed me how she always kept a kettle of water hot on a hook hanging over the fire. She roasted potatoes in the wood ashes and rested a frying pan on an iron trivet over coals when she had bacon or other meat to fry. She baked cornbread in the same iron skillet, setting it directly on a bed of ashes just hot enough to bake the bread without burning it.

Outside, they showed us where they planned to build their house and which bushes and trees they would keep in the yard. Anna Mae had designed the house they would build, and she asked Monroe, who had taken a course in mechanical drawing while he was in the navy, to make a scale drawing of it for them. While we were discussing their plans, their young daughter, Edna V., came back from taking some of Anna Mae's just-baked bread to her great-grandmother up the road.

The next Monday we drove the fifty miles back up to Brasstown to see what kind of job there could be for Monroe at the Folk School. We observed many changes at the school in the four years we had been away. The school had very few students and was recovering from being shorthanded during the war years. Mrs. Campbell, her health in decline, was now living in New England near her family. Louise Pitman still traveled often to the Northeast, arranging future craft sales for the Folk School. Meetings of the Southern Highland Handicraft Guild that she and Olive Campbell had been instrumental in forming often required Louise to be in Asheville. Marguerite and Georg Bidstrup continued to play leading roles in the day-to-day running of the school. Eva Mae Henson, secretary in the school office, helped keep everyone organized.

The carvers still came weekly and brought their work for finishing and sale by the school. Many of the carvers had made some changes in their patterns, and there were some totally new carving designs. Jack Hall continued to carve his windblown horses in a realistic stance, but others were carving more stylized horses. Murray Martin continued to design, critique, and teach the community carvers, as well as teaching regular courses in carving and weaving at the school as she had been doing since 1935.

For convenience, the weaving room had been moved into Keith House from the small room next to the laundry. The woodworking shop had burned in the third year of the war, so the finishing and shipping of the carvings and weavings moved to an upstairs room in Keith House.

Fannie McClellan was in charge of craft sales at the school. She now had the tasks of putting clear finishes on the carvings and filling orders for the school's crafts. That meant that my old job at the school was already filled, but Marguerite was sure they could find something else for me to do. She suggested that I could learn to weave the wool runners and place mats Murray designed for sale in Boston, Washington, and Philadelphia. Georg told Monroe they could make him the "foreman in the field." He would no longer be milking cows, but he would be able to learn more about biodynamic farming, a relatively new concept that employed only organic materials for fertilizing and soil conditioning.

The school would furnish an apartment for us on the upper floor of Hill House. We would both have jobs and a place to live! I was overjoyed at the prospect of having indoor plumbing, two paychecks, and the stimulation of the Folk School's intellectual and creative environment. Monroe was also pleased with the opportunity to enroll under the G.I. Bill in the woodworking course to be taught soon by Herman Estes. We agreed that we could probably start early in March as soon as we completed our visit with Monroe's family.

Encouraged and happy, we drove back to Hemp and gave the good news to Mama Wilson. She was glad we had found work so soon. The family's tradition of valuing good work habits was alive and strong. She also knew that we would be close enough to come for Sunday dinner often. Satisfied about our future, we resumed life in "Hemptown." As I helped with the cooking and cleaning up after meals, my mother-in-law told me her story bit by bit.

When Letha Leowa Mashburn was ten years old, she dropped out of school in Hemp. She had learned all that was offered in this two-room school: reading, writing, and arithmetic. She could figure any number problem in her head, read anything that made its way into her hands, and write to anyone in the family who might venture far enough away to want to hear from her. At home, her mother needed help with the younger children, the housework, and the cooking.

Letha set about the practical business of everyday living: sewing, cooking, washing, ironing, gardening, preserving food, and caring for people. By twenty-one, she brought all these necessary skills into her marriage to Herman Everett Wilson, the only son of a prominent family in Hemp. Children arrived regularly, and after a number of her own were delivered, Letha Leowa learned to help other women deliver their babies when the doctor was slow to arrive. She became a midwife and a community authority on medicinal plants; searching for them in the woods and fields, hanging them to dry, and storing them until they were needed.

Mama Wilson told me that when she was a young woman in 1901, someone asked how she managed to accomplish all that she needed to do with a husband and rapidly growing family. She replied cheerfully that early on she knew she had to hurry and she intended to hurry from then on. As each of her ten babies entered the world, she managed to find some task to keep the others busy. An infant held the attention of those a little older and so was useful in keeping them out of mischief. Toddlers managed to shoo the chickens away from the garden. Older children had suitable chores to do. So it went until the work ethic was firmly planted in each family member.

No one ever knew exactly how many quilts Letha made in her lifetime, but it would have been a tall pile. Prior to marriage, she had pieced and quilted as many as she would need in the future for her own household. A quilt frame was hoisted up to the ceiling of the front room, ready to be lowered and used whenever a quilting bee was in order. There was usually a quilt in progress, waiting to honor a special occasion.

As the four oldest girls grew, they also learned to sew and help with the quilting. Mama Wilson made twelve quilts and a feather bed for each of her daughters. For her sons, she provided six quilts and a feather bed for the bedstead their father gave them as a wedding present. After she completed these responsibilities, Mama—now Grandma—Wilson started making quilts for the grandchildren. Using traditional patterns, she stitched Dutch doll quilts for little girls, fans or bow ties for the baby boys.

This tradition of work was well rooted in several generations of hardy pioneers who came to the mountains of northwest Georgia from parts of Scotland and England in the early 1700s. Whenever the Wilson family got together and welcomed a newcomer into the circle of family or friends, the hymn of praise would echo: "She's a good worker . . . she does a good job . . . there's nothing lazy about that man . . . he knows how to work." I felt that I met these criteria and was grateful for Mama Wilson's acceptance and for the sense of kinship I gained as I became a part of this family of my heart.

BUILDING A FUTURE

In March 1946, we drove up to Brasstown from Hemp in our trusty old Rosie, which was loaded with all our earthly possessions. The inventory was greatly enhanced with practical wedding presents from each member of Monroe's family: new quilts, home-canned applesauce and beans, jellies and jams, a jar of honey, a huge bag of potatoes, and other food supplies.

We stopped at Keith House and found Eva Mae Henson, who gave us a happy welcome and the key to the upstairs apartment at Hill House. We had a private side entrance that led to a long flight of stairs up to the apartment. Downstairs Cecil and Alice Holland Tipton lived in the two-bedroom apartment with their four small children. Cecil worked on the school farm and Alice helped Miss Gaines in the kitchen. They would soon be moving to their own house on their farm in Brasstown across Highway 64.

Our apartment was already partially furnished as temporary housing for occasional school visitors and members of the board of directors—now it was ours. We had no furniture of our own and explored with interest what had been provided. At the top of the stairs was the kitchen. It featured a three-burner oil stove and a portable oven to place on one of the burners if we wanted to bake. For mealtime there was a very low table flanked with two straight chairs. It graced one corner of the kitchen under high windows that looked out over the driveway below. The large living room had four windows facing across fields toward the beautiful blue mountains to the west. At the end of a central hallway was a large bedroom with high windows and twin beds. The small, dark bathroom was halfway between the bedroom and the kitchen.

In the living room a cot covered with an India-print bedspread served as couch and extra bed. There were assorted straight chairs and a comfortable wooden rocker, as well as two small tables with electric lights converted from old oil lamps. Here and there a pottery ashtray or vase completed the decor.

Soon a wonderful variety of gifts and good wishes arrived from friends and relatives who had recently received our marriage announcements. They understood that we had not had time to send out wedding invitations because of the short notice of Monroe's leave and our departure for North Carolina. Even our wedding portrait wasn't photographed until the next summer—very typical of wartime weddings.

Mother sent my small, antique, walnut chest of drawers by Railway Express. I put it in the hallway at the top of the stairs to serve as a greeting to visitors. I arranged a potted plant, a small lamp, and a guest book on it and put a mirror over it for last-minute checks of my appearance as I left the apartment. Even Marguerite was impressed with my interior decorating.

Aunt Lucy sent a beautiful mahogany bed that had belonged to her first mother-in-law and dated back to the mid-1800s. We were surprised to find that the mattress, resting on wooden slats, was very short and was pieced out with a second section of mattress at the bottom of the bed. Aunt Lucy had explained to Mother that at that time people were generally shorter. Most families used corn-shuck mattresses on their beds, so her mother-in-law was very pleased to have a real mattress, and it was a good length for her. Our first purchase was a proper mattress from the new Ivie's furniture store in Murphy. It was nice to add two real antiques to our furnishings, and good also to have something to remind us of Aunt Lucy's generosity throughout the years.

Aunt Lucy was ten years old when my mother, Florence Olney, was born in Rome, New York, in 1889. Throughout their childhood Lucy played with her little cousin Florence as with a doll. Mother remained very close to Aunt Lucy in spite of physical distance between them. Aunt Lucy was very wealthy, traveled to Europe, and spent winters in Florida.

During my childhood she was married three times. Uncle Bert, her first husband, was a close friend of my father and introduced him to mother. After her first husband died, Aunt Lucy married Uncle Bill Kingsley. He was the tallest man I had ever seen. When they visited us at our home on Long Island, he had to duck to go through any doorway in the house. He and Aunt Lucy came to visit us one Easter, bringing the most beautiful Easter cake I have ever seen. There were prizes hidden in almost every slice of cake. One of the treasures was a five-dollar gold piece. As Easter presents they brought each of us girls a gold charm bracelet with a special charm. Barbara's was a coral Buddha, mine had a gold elephant, and Louise's had a small gold squirrel. We didn't see Aunt Lucy again for several years.

Uncle Bill lost a great deal of money in the stock market crash of 1929. He was so filled with despair at his failure to invest his money safely that he ended his life by jumping out of the window on the top floor of a skyscraper in Florida. After Aunt Lucy married a third time, she continued to surprise us every once in a while with very generous gifts.

As soon as we were settled in our apartment in Hill House, we both started work for the school. I walked over to Keith House each morning and wove wool runners with Christine Hyatt, who had been weaving for the Folk School all through the war years. She was expert in threading a loom and in designing runners woven from vegetable-dyed wool. She taught me how to wind bobbins and thread a warp. We wove together day after day, concentrating on the pattern and only talking with each other when it was time to take a short break.

Christine lived with her mother two miles away on Settawig Road in Brasstown and left in midafternoon to walk home. I often continued to practice weaving after we had finished for the day. I loved the rhythm of weaving but found it difficult at first to keep the edges even. Murray gave me permission to practice on a loom that was already threaded and suitable for linen or cotton place mats and short runners. I experimented with a blue patterned stripe on a white cotton background and was pleased to see how even small variations made interesting changes in the design. I kept the striped rows to remind me of design possibilities. Murray told me flatly that it was not a design, just a sampler, but to this day, it is one of my favorite small pieces. It was my pleasure to weave Christmas presents for all my extended family the first year of our marriage.

Monroe planted spring crops and was also busy with the wonderful opportunities for handicrafts that the school offered. His first project in the woodworking shop was a dining table to replace the low one we were using in Hill House. He chose to make it with lumber of maple and poplar in a plain Shaker design. It was just the right height for the two maple chairs that he finished to go with the table.

On recommendation from Herman Estes, we located Mr. Woody's house on the road to Martins Creek. Mr. Woody wove oak split seats for all sorts of chairs, and we knew his seats would give a beautiful finish to our breakfast set. When we went to pick them up and pay him, he was kind and was pleased to meet a student and new craftsman at the school. We felt accepted in the community, greatly encouraged, and happily accepted the student discount he offered.

Georg allotted a garden plot to us next to the school's kitchen garden. As the days grew longer, we walked over after work to tend the garden. Monroe laughed at my awkwardness and gave up trying to show me how to cultivate the seedlings, but I gradually became adept at wielding a hoe. Then the care of the garden fell to me. Those first green onions and tender leaves of turnip greens tasted mighty fine!

As spring came to the mountains, some of Monroe's family came to eat dinner with us one Sunday afternoon. We set up a folding table under the oak trees on the side lawn and carried down chairs. I had baked a cake and Boston baked beans. I still hadn't mastered the art of biscuit making, so I relied on the muffin recipe I had used several times when I was living with the Taylors in Cambridge. Monroe's family thought they were cupcakes, but ate them appreciatively with the meal. It was a pleasant time enjoying family and christening our home.

Olive Campbell had returned from Massachusetts to spend the summer at Farm House as was her custom. Despite small strokes that plagued her and frightened me, she was her generous self. While Mama Wilson was spending a weekend with us, Mrs. Campbell decided it would be polite to invite the three of us for Sunday night supper at Farm House. The two ladies were about the same age, and both had always loved these mountains.The three of us walked over from Hill House at suppertime as the sun sank lower in the sky beyond the hay barn.

Mrs. Campbell welcomed us all with courtly elegance at the kitchen door. After exchanging introductions and greetings, Mrs. Campbell showed us to a small table beside an open fire on the hearth in the room next to the kitchen where she usually had her breakfast and tea. Monroe and his mother sat down, while Mrs. Campbell and I put the finishing touches on a large batch of her customary Sunday evening waffles. I arranged the sausages with a waffle on each plate and carried the plates to our places. There was a large bowl of homemade applesauce, a generous pitcher of maple syrup, and hot tea to drink.

The two ladies made polite conversation, and we knew enough not to interfere except when further explanations were called for, as they sometimes were. There was a decided difference in the colloquial expressions each used. It was a delightful meal, a gracious blending of two cultures and the meeting of two wonderful women.

As we walked home, I asked Mama Wilson if she had enjoyed herself. I wish I could recall her polite words exactly, but I do remember her compassionate tone of voice, "Poor dear," Mama Wilson said, "she did the best she could, didn't she? I've never had a waffle for dinner before, but they were good, weren't they?" Visions of Letha's Sunday dinner table, covered with heaping bowls of vegetables, several platters of meat, and a huge layer cake came to my mind. I smiled happily as I recognized the grace of these two fine ladies of years gone by.

I wove for the Folk School for a year and loved that work, but I didn't feel I was artistic enough to do it for the rest of my life. My place in the Folk School family had changed during the war years, in keeping with all the other changes that had occurred. I no longer felt needed. The Folk School itself was slowly changing.

For me, the most serious of the changes at the Folk School was the imminent retirement of Olive Campbell, my friend, a former housemate, and my inspiration. She was spending less time in Brasstown as she worked toward returning to Massachusetts to live near her family. Trying to ease the school into transition by helping to choose a new director, Mrs. Campbell had appealed to the Folk School board of directors for help in finding a suitable replacement.

Since the origin of the school in 1929, there had been a governing board of directors. They had largely financed the beginnings of the school and continued to provide advice and support, meeting regularly twice each year. The original group was made up of responsible people "from away," including friends of the Bidstrups from Ohio, and relatives and friends of Mrs. Campbell's from Massachusetts. They were a dedicated group of people who made decisions on school programs, personnel, and budget with the best interests of the Folk School in mind. The board supported the original goals of the school to serve the people of the rural mountains. For several years different members volunteered to live in Brasstown to more directly guide the school.

A series of very capable leaders followed for short periods of time. In each interim between trials, the school was fortunate to have Georg and Marguerite Bidstrup at the helm. They were planning to build their own house on a hill in Brasstown as soon as possible. Marguerite had been designing and planning furnishings, and they looked forward to freedom from the full-time responsibility of the school, but they were willing to fill in as needed.

In spite of the many changes occurring, we still had good friends at the school. Miss Gaines loved to have me stop by her room or visit with her on the kitchen porch, and she continued to be my close friend. Our second big purchase after the mattress for our bed was a radio so we could listen to the news at night. We found just what we wanted in Murphy and were so proud of our small Philco that we stopped at Keith House and invited Miss Gaines to come over and listen to the news with us. It was the first of many times we kidnapped her from her second-floor room to keep us company and observe our progress in homemaking.

Change was also coming to the region as a whole. The war and travel to countries "across the water" had helped to make our community less isolated. There were more opportunities for local people made possible through new government programs such as the G.I. Bill for veteran education. There were now jobs here as well as in Ohio or Atlanta. Small farming was no longer the primary source of income but a supplement to life in the country. I began to look for ways in which I could work in the Brasstown community rather than at the Folk School.

New Opportunities

When we first went back to Brasstown after visiting with Monroe's family in Georgia, I visited postmistress Mrs. Iowa Green. Subsequently I again began to substitute for her whenever she needed me. In the same way I had when I was in charge of taking the Folk School mail to the post office, I worked with her to decipher the government communications she received periodically. With each succeeding year they became more frequent and more complex and obscure. They were usually just form letters written in trite bureaucratic language, but because they were on official stationery, she always worried that they contained important information. My experience at the Rockefeller Foundation during the war made the language very familiar to me.

During the rush of Christmas mail, I helped in the post office part time to give Mrs. Green time to walk to her house to fix lunch for her elderly mother and her bachelor brother. It felt good for me to have a friend in such an important position in the community. Mrs. Green's grown son was in Atlanta. Her daughter was in college in Berea, Kentucky, so Mrs. Green enjoyed having a substitute daughter helping her.

The next year Monroe and I moved from Hill House to a drafty little old house near the barns. He had been transferred from his position as foreman in the field to being in charge of the school dairy again. This house was closer to his early morning work of milking thirty-nine purebred Jersey cows and two large Holsteins. I set about making it a home.

I planted daffodils along the sporadic flagstone path down to the road. Across the road in front of the house there was a fenced area that would be perfect for a garden, but someone had planted black walnuts with the intent of starting an orchard. The saplings sent out roots which discouraged growth near them, so we had to sacrifice the young trees in order to have a vegetable garden. Their slim young trunks made good firewood for the many open fireplaces that provided the only heat in the house.

For the kitchen, we again went to Ivie's furniture store in Murphy and bought a wood cookstove. To the right of the four stove eyes there was a tank that held and heated water. We would be able to dip it out into a bucket to use for baths and dishwashing.

Mother had written to complain that she was having difficulty taking care of Mr. Chips, the golden cocker spaniel we bought in Maine for Louise's birthday just before she went off to college. Louise had had to leave Mr. Chips in Cedarhurst when she married and moved to Louisiana, and I had enjoyed him for the year I was at home. I could not bear to think of Mother's getting rid of him and told her that I would be delighted to have him. She promptly sent him down to me by Railway Express.

Monroe wanted to have a truck as soon as any became available after the war, so we sold our faithful Ford in Copperhill, Tennessee. Because the fumes from the copper-smelting plant there caused cars to rust quickly, there was a good market for used cars from elsewhere. We took the money from the sale of Rosie to buy one of the first trucks to come on the market in Murphy. We loved our new red GMC pickup truck. After we bought our new stove, loaded it on our truck, and installed it at home, I returned to the railway depot in Murphy to meet "Chipsie" and take him home.

In the afternoons Monroe studied woodworking with Herman Estes. A new woodworking shop had been built especially for creating and finishing small furniture, such as the nests of small tables made from native hardwoods that the school sold. When the TVA cleared some farm orchards and vast acres of woodland to make way for the building of lakes and power plants, the school had been able to buy ample supplies of apple, holly, wild cherry, maple, and black walnut timber. It had been sawed, dried in the school's dry kiln, and stacked in the lumberyard.

One of Monroe's early furniture-building projects was a cherry drop-leaf dining table for our new home. He brought it home for me to finish. I sanded it endlessly until it was silky smooth, then covered it with countless coats of sheen coat finish, and buffed it at last into smoothness that would endure for at least sixty years. As soon as that was done, he presented me with a corner cupboard to match, and I repeated the procedure. Next he built a Welsh dresser and six ladder-back chairs with carved acorn finials on top to match the feet of the table. How pleased we were with our dining-room furniture, and how proud we were when Monroe ultimately achieved the rank of master craftsman in woodworking!

Both Monroe and I had spent our childhood in the throes of the Great Depression. We were afraid of poverty and dependence. I spent a good deal of time while I was waiting for the war to end reading a book about subsistence farming, *Roots in the Earth*. I was convinced that we could have a good and safe life on a small farm. The Folk School taught all the skills necessary to create an interesting home in the pioneer style. It was a good time for us as we worked toward that goal.

We each had work we enjoyed and spent time with friends both at the school and in the community. We continued to go often to Keith House and to the Friday Night Games, and we stayed in touch with school staff when we visited the library or gift shop. From time to time some students walked down the hill and spent a bit of "home time" with us. Of course, Monroe both worked and studied at the Folk School, but we always enjoyed hearing others' views to keep us up to date.

One summer day in 1948, Douglas Smith, the principal of Martins Creek School, stopped at the house to ask me if I would teach the seventh grade there. They had sufficient enrollment to add another teacher to the six already busy teaching eight grades. As principal, Mr. Smith was too busy with administration and teaching both seventh and eighth grades to take on more teaching duties. I happily accepted the position.

It was a year of wonderful learning for me. I rode to school early each morning with Douglas and his first-grade daughter, Patsy. I usually came home on the school bus late in the afternoon. The day was filled with all that country schools offered. For better or worse, I taught all that was required and more, whenever and whatever, as I pleased. I was well prepared for the academic material but somewhat unsure of the extracurricular activities. Students in the seventh grade ranged in age from twelve to sixteen; I remember each and every one of them.

I refereed girls' softball, suffering the slings and arrows of catcalls and boos if I was wrong in my decisions. I also supervised the students during lunch. We all carried trays from the lunchroom to eat a balanced diet at our desks in the classroom. Once a week I taught art, encouraging careful observation of nature as we searched for objects to draw through the windows or in desktop still lifes. The class was amazed to observe that tree trunks are not solid brown in color but a shaded mixture of tan, black, and dark gray.

To provide a music class, I counted on the youngest member of the class, Jerry Ruth Smith. She could play the piano and several small instruments and could lead the singing without any accompaniment. She gradually overcame her shyness and grew to enjoy being a leader. The class chose songs they knew and loved, and we made music that my tone deafness couldn't spoil.

I loved the academic subjects—reading, writing, history, geography, and mathematics—as well as the responsibility of preparing the students for high school life. Every day after lunch I read to the class from a classic such as Rudyard Kipling's *Jungle Book*. Students had the option of putting their heads on their desks and napping if they preferred that to listening. I enjoyed the relief of a good story to break up the day.

In diverse and subtle ways the class taught me more than I taught them. There were still many descendants of the early Scots-Irish families who settled in the mountains, bearing names like Chapman, Mashburn, and Boyd. Some of the pronunciations unfamiliar to me could be traced to these roots.

One of the younger boys, a towhead who was only twelve, missed a day of school and came back with the excuse that his calf had pneumonia, and he had to stay home to take care of it. I thought he was making a joke about his absence. I had no idea that animals ever had pneumonia, and I laughed at him. Soberly he explained that it was a very serious illness in animals, and he was hoping his calf would recover.

One of the brightest girls in the class missed two days of school because she had only one pair of shoes. When she came back she told me that she hated to miss even one day of school, but her shoe had to go for sole repair, and she couldn't go barefoot in the winter. It was a revelation to me that anyone could manage with only one pair of shoes.

Luke, the eldest in the class, was a tall Native American who had played truant so often through the years that he had hardly learned to read, despite his above-average intelligence. Now in the seventh grade, he taught himself to read fluently by repeatedly reading the driver's education manual so that on his sixteenth birthday he would be eligible to get his permit for a driver's license.

On one rainy afternoon we were all confined to our room for recess because the younger grades were playing in the auditorium. Our free time became seriously rowdy, and I implored the class to "calm down and stop acting like wild Indians." Luke stepped up behind me. In his manly gruff voice he boomed, "Indians are not wild!" I apologized and learned to be more watchful of my stereotypes.

School days from eight in the morning until four in the afternoon were long, but variety put spice in the hours. We observed all the holidays in multiple ways. By midwinter I was an expert—both at school and after hours at home—in making cookies, cutting and pasting homemade cards, and experimenting with other frills for school celebrations. Of course I went all out to get ready for Valentine's Day: cards and cookies for everyone in the class! We had a great time playing games, exchanging greetings, singing, and telling stories.

After the Valentine's Day celebration I was exhausted. I was the last person remaining on the school bus that day when it finally stopped in front of our house. I hurried up the front walk and opened the door into the quiet, empty living room. Surprise! I was greeted with a small walnut rocking chair festooned with many strings of cutout red paper hearts. Propped on the seat was a huge heart lettered "With love from Monroe." In his spare time he had been working on this new creation, complete with a fiber-cord woven seat, ready for rocking. Imagine that he'd once said he didn't believe in celebrating holidays!

I think Monroe hoped I would teach every year forever, but he certainly did not tell me that was his plan. Many families on small farms supplemented their income by having one person teach during the school year, but that wasn't my idea—I wanted to farm instead. In late March of 1949, Monroe came home one evening and announced that we could buy Gwen and Harriet Cornwell's farm with the money I had saved in the years I taught in New York City and this year at Martins Creek.

It was spring, school would soon be over, and we would begin planting a garden again. Chipsie enjoyed walking along the road in front of our house as he followed Monroe to work at the barn. One morning there was a car accident, and he was killed. My grief was not abated by Herman Estes' gift of a little, dark red, female cocker spaniel puppy named Sandy. We had planned a marriage for her with Chipsie and hoped to raise puppies to sell, but we had to bury Mr. Chips on the hill behind the house. We hated to leave him behind, but we had all kinds of reasons for wanting to leave Folk School property for a place of our own. When Monroe told me that the Cornwells' farm in "downtown Brasstown." was for sale, we were both interested and ready to explore various possibilities.

FARM LIFE

꧁❦꧂

The daffodils along our walkway at the house near the barns were blooming prettily. We had been back at the Folk School for three years and were talking often about woodworking, farming, and independence. We had considered living in a number of different places in the mountains where we already knew other couples, but we were most interested in living in Brasstown. We decided to consider purchasing the Cornwell farm.

Already there were several couples who had completed the Folk School program and had settled on farms near Brasstown. Among them were Wayne and Gladys Holland, Fred and Ruth Smith, Sue and Hickory Reece, Frank and Bea Hogan, Blanche and Douglas Smith, Robert and Virginia Anderson, as well as a number of young couples who had been born and raised in Brasstown and had resisted the temptation to seek their fortunes outside the mountains. Most were farming at least part time and raising their families there.

I had watched as Gwen and Harriet Cornwell's house was being built in 1941 when I first came to Brasstown. Their farm was on the hill above the Brasstown Post Office, in the center of Brasstown across Old Route 64 and Brasstown Creek from the Folk School property. The farm's pasture and cropland stretched out gently uphill along Green Cove Road and across toward woodland bordering Old Route 64, to the west and south of the house.

An old barn, corn crib, and abandoned well were part of the property that had been there since before the turn of the century. A rutted road tracked between open fields from the ruins of an abandoned Methodist church on the corner of Green Cove and Creamery roads to an old Scroggs family cemetery dating back to the last century. Gwen and Harriet had bought the farm before the war from a member of the Scroggs family, who moved away to find work elsewhere. When Gwen returned from the war, he built a beautiful big dairy barn, a fine new garage, and laid down two concrete strips to serve as a driveway up the hill from Settawig Road.

We drove over the following Saturday after Monroe had finished milking and found both Gwen and Harriet at home, ready to show us around. Gwen met us in the yard at the top of the hill. He explained that the garage now held a huge purebred boar, named Eichenhauer (a name similar to the President's, although not exactly the same, so they shared the nickname Ike). The huge beast was a valuable asset for breeding the best possible pigs for us and our neighbors each year. They would be pigs easy to fatten, with good lean meat and plenty of lard with which to cook. "You know," Gwen said, "everyone fattens at least one hog every year. So we've turned the garage into a piggery with birthing pens for the sows and a special high stall for Ike." At that point we could hear the boar's incessant roar.

Gwen suggested we join Harriet inside to tour the house. The house was not finished on the outside. The walls were covered with black tar paper between the studs, ready for a natural rock veneer when they could afford it, Gwen explained. He ushered us into the house through the small screened back porch that led to the kitchen on the left. The kitchen had a wood cookstove, plenty of counter space, and two built-in bins to hold flour and cornmeal. Ahead was a small room that now served as Gwen's farm office. Harriet suggested that it would make a nice dining room for our cherry furniture.

The living room had built-in bookcases on both sides of a large stone fireplace, a front door that looked out over the steep hill below, and a side glass door that opened onto an unfinished terrace. There were two bedrooms and a small half-finished bathroom, all opening off a short central hallway. Stairs from the hall in back of the chimney led down to a spacious basement.

The cellar floor was covered with cinder ashes except for a section of finished concrete under a tall bank of incubators in one corner. It filled one fourth of the entire space under the house. Gwen explained that the incubating eggs were already beginning to hatch, so we needed to talk quietly so as not to disturb the fledgling chicks. He would sell the baby chicks and the incubators to Mountain Valley Cooperative next week when they settled up for the milk Gwen marketed there.

This reminded us of the fact that we were thinking about buying a working dairy farm, not just a home, in Brasstown. We needed to see all that this business involved, so we went up to the big barn and examined the milking parlor. There were six or seven stanchions in front of the feeding trough and a pipeline to attach milking machines. The adjacent small room had washtubs and a huge electric cooler. Outside the barn, waiting to go out to pasture, was the dairy herd. There were five cows—two huge registered Holsteins, two registered Jerseys, and Old Red—plus a number of yearlings and calves. Gwen told us that the farm was well fenced; he thought it was even safe for the young pigs to graze in the pasture below the piggery. He pointed out the three long fields beyond the barn. He usually turned the cows out to graze in the middle field, planted corn in another, and cut hay from the third that was currently planted in alfalfa. As he had learned to do while at the Folk School, Gwen rotated the fields each year.

We went back to the house and sat at the kitchen table to talk about all we had seen. I was really anxious to try subsistence farming and was impressed by the number of enterprising projects Gwen had undertaken on this fifty-acre farm. I saw all sorts of possibilities for carrying on a busy farm life right in the heart of Brasstown. The house was unfinished, but even as it was, it was quite charming. The pine-paneled walls were attractive, the hardwood floors were pretty, the fireplace was beautiful. There was plenty of room for us, with opportunities to expand. We had learned much at the Folk School that we could put to use here.

In addition to the land, buildings, and livestock, the farm carried with it membership in a machine co-op and credit union. The co-op's toolshed where the machines were stored was here, and Monroe would be in charge of maintenance of the equipment and keeping records of where each was being used. I saw a lot of positives in the prospect of buying this place.

Harriet murmured apologetically that there was no spectacular view, but I didn't care. I was satisfied with near views of fields and woods. I didn't know what Monroe thought of the place, but he seemed interested. I had great faith in his knowledge of farming and trusted him completely. I had saved money ever since we met, and I was ready to invest in the farm as I had already invested in him.

We both were reasonably intelligent, but neither of us had ever been in business or in debt. We did not know the business aspects of farming, so when Harriet and Gwen offered to take our down payment and finance the loan themselves, with a payment from us each year for twelve years, we felt that their confidence in us was reassuring. As we left, we thanked the Cornwells for the tour and assured them that we would talk it over and let them know our decision.

That evening Monroe didn't talk much about how he felt about buying the farm or what he thought of it. It was always difficult to get him to talk about his opinions. I knew that it was a great place, and I was excited and pleased. I felt that the house would be as attractive and pleasant when we moved into it as it was now with Harriet's things. I loved the thought of being in the middle of Brasstown. At that time many people in the area did not even have electricity and certainly not an indoor bathroom; I was excited at the thought of all we would have. Realistically, however, we had no idea how many gallons of milk we might be selling or what the price of milk was at this time—we hadn't asked. Could we make the yearly payments from the proceeds of the farm? We talked about it and thought about all that was included. Monroe didn't seem to doubt that we could manage. I was eager to learn and help. Only in retrospect can I see that our expectations of ourselves, each other, and of the farm were unrealistic; but we were young and our hopes were high. Sixty years later I can say, "Thank God for giving us the courage to take a chance!"

We signed the papers and waited while Harriet and Gwen moved to Murphy. Then we took responsibility for the farm, gradually carrying our furnishings over, one pickup-load at a time. The first evening we planned to spend the night in our own house, we were alerted by neighbors that our young pigs had left our land to go to the field along Brasstown Creek across Highway 64. That field belonged to Ruth and Hilliard Logan, who with several other neighbors, kindly helped us round up the pigs. The expression pigheaded takes on new meaning once you have tried to coax or drive a pig in a direction he doesn't choose to go. I certainly gained new respect for their determination as we worked to round up that wayward pork. There was relief when at last we managed to close them up in one of the barns to keep them out of trouble until we could mend the fence and make it hog proof! It was reassuring to find that we had neighbors who would come to our rescue when we needed help. We were glad to be in this close community.

Saturday night, however, was a different matter altogether. A vacant corner lot below our place was community property, with a spring from which anyone could draw water. The lot was fenced and used by the men in the community to hold horses and cattle that they planned to sell in Murphy at the next public auction. On Saturday nights the men gathered to feed and water the animals they were holding but also to celebrate together. From the sounds of merriment, we gathered that there was plenty of liquid refreshment for men as well as beasts. The revelry went on through the evening and into the night, and it was still resounding at midnight.

We had closed our windows but still heard a piercing shriek coming from a house across the road, "Jim, Jim, come on home! It's late and I'm going to bed. Jim, Jim, you hear me? Come on home right now or I'll come and get you." Silence for a bit, then another voiced called, "Fred O.! Come on home. It's time to quit for the night." Then again, "Jim, Jim! I'm coming, you'd better get in here." Eventually all the merriment below us quieted. The wives had called off the party for the night.

We gradually came to know everyone within earshot, and doubtless they knew us as well. Pearl Adams from across the street came to visit and said she really enjoyed my whistling as I went about work at the barn. She thought I could sing in the church choir and wanted me to give it a try; she didn't know that I'm practically tone deaf.

Mae and Alla Scroggs walked up one afternoon with their flow-erpots in hand. They stopped at the house and said they had always used the woods dirt under the trees in back of our house. Did I mind if they filled their flowerpots again today? The good black dirt was perfect for the cuttings they had from their houseplants. Of course I welcomed them then and again another week when they walked up through the yard and across the pasture above the house to visit the graves in the old family cemetery on the top of the hill. It was good to have neighbors visiting freely.

My friend Mrs. Green welcomed us to the neighborhood when she visited her mother, one-hundred-year-old Granny Beach, who lived near us on Green Cove Road. Soon after we moved to our farm, Granny Beach died. It was customary in the country for the undertaker to come and take the body to prepare it for burial while the family to choose a casket; then the funeral director would bring the body back to the house to await burial from there.

Early on after I came to the South, I learned that people here express their sympathy in deeds as often as with words. When I first heard of a death I always baked a layer cake. Ours was part of a parade of cakes to Mrs. Green's house that was already full of friends, relatives, and neighbors talking and enjoying each other's company. When night fell and the crowd in the small living room thinned, Mrs. Green asked who was able to stay the night to sit vigil with the body. The open casket rested in state under the windows. Monroe and I volunteered. Having done our farm chores early, there was no reason that we had to go home. We spent a long, quiet night with Granny Beach, peaceful and undisturbed. The bookcase was filled with Reader's Digest Condensed Books. We read most of the night as we became comfortable with death. Our presence in the house was appreciated by the family, and we were thankful to be able to help.

My first major responsibility on the farm was to watch the sows as they gave birth to piglets. If interrupted in the process, a sow might roll over and crush her infant pigs, so I needed to be sure that nothing disturbed her. We were rewarded with several good litters of piglets. They ran in the pasture, and I laughed with pleasure as I observed them race along the open field. Suddenly one would come to a stop to rest flat on his stomach for a minute before he was off again like the wind. Pigs definitely have personalities, and I thoroughly enjoyed getting to know them. We sold them to neighbors as fast as they were old enough, and their days of freedom ended in fattening pens. We kept several to fatten and send to market and one to grow fat enough to butcher for our own wonderful meals.

Butchering a hog usually took place on Thanksgiving Day. Monroe shot the hog in the head and then cut its throat. With the help of a neighbor he hoisted the hog, head down, on a pole stretched between two small dogwood trees in the yard above the house. With a sharp knife Monroe split it open down the belly. Then he removed the heart, liver, and gizzard; and brought them in a dishpan to the house for me to cook. We feasted on pork chops and ribs or canned them in glass jars for the winter. The hams and shoulders were salted down, some flat slabs were cured into bacon, and all were kept in a sawdust-filled box. Scraps were ground and seasoned for sausage. There was plenty of meat for the year to come. Monroe cut the fat into chunks, and I put it in the biggest pot I had and heated it all to a boiling point to render the fat into lard for cooking.

It took us a while to learn about all of the other animals on our farm. There was a large old farm horse who objected to work but loved to roam the pasture. Monroe needed him to plow the garden in a fenced acre on the far side of the big barn. Unfortunately the horse had an inherent sense of when he would be asked to work, and he evaded any encounter with someone holding a bridle. It was my job to hide in the milk room and watch for him to go into the stall in the old barn where I had put a scoop of delicious oats in his trough. When he found it, went in, and put his head down to nibble, I ran across the opening between barns and slammed the door on the stall while he was enjoying dinner. The next day Monroe would hitch him up to the plow, and he'd do a bit of work for us.

The cows were not usually contrary, but they enjoyed routine. They preferred that Monroe call them in from the field. They became stubborn if he were late in coming home and I tried to get them in. Granny was the big purebred Holstein, largely white with black spots. After leading the other cows into the milking barn, she was the cow who gave buckets of milk willingly into the milking machine. She had no difficulty finding her place and allowing the stanchion to be fastened around her neck. Creamelle was our other registered Holstein. We had planned to build a herd of registered Holsteins with her but were disappointed when her first calf, whom we named Frosty, was of obviously mixed heritage.

We also had two Jersey cows from the Folk School herd. Their milk was rich in butterfat but not as plenteous as that of Granny and Creamelle. Harriet was one Jersey, and the other was Minnie, an innate wanderer. No fence could hold her. The best we could do was to eventually sell her to a neighbor with good fences. There were also several half-grown heifers and Old Red who was gentle and easy to milk. All the animals had idiosyncratic personalities, so it was easy to become as fond of them as if they were pets instead of our tickets to a livelihood. Monroe was adept at milking and took charge of the cows, but I certainly did my share of washing up after we finished milking.

I was also in charge of feeding the calves. We took them away from their mothers soon after they were born. The little heifers were treated royally. Until they were grown, they were fed milk from a special bucket that had a nipple attached to a spout. Then until they were expectant mothers, they ate the most nutritious mash we could afford. The little bull calves were sold as soon as they could be weaned from milk, but we always kept one to fatten.

On a cold day in autumn Monroe built a fire in the yard and killed the yearling calf he had been fattening. He dressed the carcass and immediately brought the heart, the liver, and the kidneys down to the house for me to cook while they were fresh. In much the same way as when he slaughtered the hog, Monroe allowed the beef to hang from a pole between two trees. Then he cut it into useable sections. The shoulders and legs would be hung to dry. Choice parts were cut into steaks, while other parts were cut into stew-sized pieces for canning. We always invited as many people as possible to come for dinner and enjoy steak week rather than can those delicious cuts and lose the tender fresh flavor of steaks and roasts. We really enjoyed celebrating steak week each fall.

We had a large assortment of chickens to supply us with eggs. Some hens laid their eggs in the hay troughs of the barn, where we could usually find a good supply to take to the house for breakfast. Some "stole out their nests," and we might not find them until all the eggs were too old to eat. Occasionally, however, a hen would be so successful in hiding her nest that she would hatch a brood of little ones. They were fun to watch from a distance. If anyone approached, the mother hen clucked the little ones together and defied anyone to come near her babies.

There were also game chickens, including some fighting roosters. Game hens laid smaller eggs with pretty mottled blue, gray, or tan shells. They were adept at hiding their nests, and there was no assurance at all that the eggs were fresh when discovered in their random hiding places. The game chickens slept in the trees above the house and were expert at waking us up in the morning. Monroe did not want to be disturbed at the first glimmer of dawn. He sent for his sister Bessie's sons, Kenneth and Lamar, to come and catch the chickens. After the fowl had all gone to roost, we watched the boys climb agilely to the top of the slender dogwood trees that surrounded the house, slip a sack over each head, and carry them off to trade away to people who raised game hens as a hobby.

It took several weeks to get settled in our animal kingdom, but we soon established a good routine and were selling milk. Every morning the Mountain Valley Cooperative milk truck drove up and took our milk cans to the creamery. As members in good standing, we attended the Mountain Valley Cooperative meetings and put whatever loose change we could spare into the credit union.

A few days after we moved onto the farm, Rufus Vick, the county farm agent, came to introduce himself and offer advice and help. He was an intelligent older agent who had worked in several counties since his graduation from agricultural college. He had come to Clay County in 1942. Nearly everyone called him Mr. Vick, out of respect for his age and experience. He had grown up in the northeastern part of the state, close to Virginia and the coast. His southern accent was different from the mountain way of speaking.

Mr. Vick was followed in a few days by his assistant, Hank

Rosenkrantz, a tall, lanky fellow who specialized in knowledge of chickens—an undertaking for which we were not quite ready. Then Velma Beam, the home agent, visited us. Velma was charming; a graduate of the Women's College in Greensboro, she had been the home demonstration agent in Clay County for five or six years.

Velma and Mr. Vick had been especially selected in Raleigh when, in the early 1940s, the system of dams and power plants was being built on the tributaries of the Tennessee River by the TVA. They were to head a team of agricultural agents that would provide educational services when the Chatuge Dam and power plant were built in Hayesville. The dam would flood the prime farmland on the Hiwassee River between North Carolina and Georgia. Farms and people would be forced to relocate. Electricity and a different style of farming would require education that the Extension Service would provide.

When Mr. Vick came to see Monroe and the cows, he usually went straight up to the barn. Afterward, he would come down to the house to visit with me. I enjoyed talking with him about farming, much as I enjoyed talking with Georg Bidstrup. I loved gardening, and Mr. Vick was helpful as I planned my large vegetable garden. Subsequently he always took an interest in how I kept the weeds under control and how the harvest was progressing.

Velma had discovered the Folk School when she first came to Clay County. She really appreciated seeing all the things Monroe and I had made for our home, and she came often to see us as we settled in. Velma and Mr. Vick were organizing the dairy farms in Clay County into a mutual support group. Each summer we all toured the dairy farms in the county on an organized trip with a special inspection of one farm that had added a new building, a piece of modern farm equipment, or a special breed of animal that the other farmers could observe. The county agents were also planning to add a Clay County Farm Fair to the list of yearly events.

In the meantime Velma began Home Demonstration Clubs in each community. At the meetings she always gave a demonstration, and I learned a great deal about housekeeping from her. She might arrange flowers for a dining table or show how to slipcover an older piece of upholstered furniture. I tried to copy her demonstrations and actually made a slipcover for my father's favorite chair that I had inherited. Members took turns hosting the monthly meetings, and I, of course, took my turn having the group at my house.

At some meetings Velma gave us information about home canning. I learned that there were two methods of preserving vegetables in glass jars. For some foods, like tomatoes or applesauce, it was possible to use a huge enamel pot with a wire rack inside to hold the jars upright and apart from each other. The pot was filled with water and the lidded filled jars were placed inside. The water was boiled for the prescribed length of time to kill any lurking germ or mold that might ruin the contents as time passed. At the end of the required time, the jars were removed and they sealed themselves as they cooled

For other vegetables and for meats, it was necessary to have a pressure cooker. Filled jars placed inside the cooker had to remain for a given time at a given pressure to kill any bacteria that might be in the contents. Velma taught us how to do these tasks safely and to preserve food from our gardens and meat from our barnyards for the year.

We were truly blessed with this team of helpers from the Extension Service, all of whom became our good friends. The team would make a great difference in our farming life and that of Clay County over the years.

FAMILIES AND FRIENDS VISIT

My mother had come every spring to visit us at the Folk School. When Monroe and I lived in the little house near the barns at the Folk School, she and Barbara drove down in their large Buick and stayed almost a week. Now, of course, Mother wanted to see our farm, so we invited her to come for a week's visit in May. When she arrived, the dogwoods were blooming on our hillside, the cornfields were plowed and ready for planting,.

As soon as we finished the morning milking, I went to the house, leaving Monroe to pour up the milk and feed the calves. Mother was still asleep. "Probably exhausted," I thought, as I remembered her face when she descended the high steps of the lone passenger car on the Southern Railway train the previous afternoon. That was the last leg of her twenty-four-hour trip from New York City to Asheville and then on to Murphy.

I took some stove wood from the green box on the back porch and, going inside, stoked the fire, filled the blue enamel coffeepot, and set it on the hottest stove eye. Then I sliced some bacon, put it in the black iron frying pan, and mixed up some biscuits. Breakfast was almost ready when Monroe came down from the barn.

Mother appeared almost simultaneously as though on cue, dressed in a spring costume of navy and white linen. She had on white tennis shoes, her concession to country life. I was glad to see that she looked rested. Mother always had a gentle birdlike energy and an anxious appealing expression. She greeted us with a happy "Good morning."

What a good sport she is, I thought, to make this pilgrimage down to see us each year. "It's so good to have you here!" I embraced her warmly. "I can't wait to show you our farm. I see you have on your walking shoes. Let's eat breakfast first. Monroe has to get back to work, but I'm going to enjoy every minute with you."

We sat down at the kitchen table and relished our current anecdotes along with biscuits and honey. As soon as we finished, Monroe pushed away from the table with a joking excuse and, retrieving his cap from the hook by the door, went back to the barn.

We stacked the dishes in the sink. Impatiently I turned and took Mother by the arm. "Oh Mother, I want to show you the cows. Monroe has probably finished washing down the milking barn and will turn the cows out to pasture soon."

"Right now?" she asked reluctantly. "I thought we'd do the dishes and make the beds and just talk."

"Please, I can't wait to show you all around," I insisted. Everything on the farm was very new and wonderful to me.

Mother was agreeable. We went up the stone steps behind the house and skirted the freshly planted vegetable garden on the path toward the farm buildings. Our cocker spaniel, Sandy, followed us happily. Jubilant with the promise of youth and springtime, I pranced ahead. "See the lettuce is up, and the English peas are blooming. I wish it were next week and you could have some. The little green onions are almost big enough too."

Mother trod carefully as we crossed the barnyard, picking her way between cow piles and muddy spots. "Dear, aren't you afraid of the cows?" she asked. "How do you know what to do with them?"

We peered into the lounging barn where I introduced Mother to our girls: Creamelle and Granny, the big Holsteins; Harriet and Minnie, our sleek Jerseys; as well as Frosty and Old Red. They were all munching their morning hay before going out to pasture. "Aren't they beautiful?" I murmured. Pride in our beginning herd completely clouded my perception of my mother's reaction.

"Over here is the pigpen," I said with a grand gesture. We turned and walked across to look over the gate across the entrance to one of the stalls in a smaller barn. A powerful stench greeted us as the two-hundred-pound body of a muddy white sow, anticipating food, rushed to her trough just inside. "This is Porky, Mother," I introduced. Mother stepped back quickly.

"Oh dear, I really don't like that smell. What in the world will you do with Porky?"

"We'll make her into delicious pork chops, sausage, bacon, ham, and lard in the fall as soon as it's cold enough," I explained with a broad smile. Mother moaned gently. Lovingly, I took her arm. We turned away from the barns and wound gently up through the edge of the hillside pasture, shaded lightly by more dogwoods in bloom."Isn't the view beautiful? We'll clear all those woods over there and turn that into pasture next year. We can use the wood for our furnace."

"But what will you do when the trees are all gone?" she asked, doubtfully.

"We'll plant more trees on the hills that we don't want to cultivate," I assured her, pointing proudly to the expanse of farm land before us. "That field will be cut for hay. It is crimson clover, planted last fall Do you want to walk out there to see the far field?"

"I think not this morning, dear. I can see it well enough for now. I don't understand how you are ever going to be able to manage all this. It seems as though it will take a lifetime."

"Maybe it will," I chirped blithely. "It's what we want to do."

As we strolled back down toward the barn I left Mother for a minute at the edge of the garden and hurried into the milk room. The clang of milk cans meant the last stages of cleanup. I leaned close to Monroe and spoke thoughtfully, "Muns, when you kill that chicken for dinner, you'd better not let Mother see you or hear it squawking."

"Don't worry," he assured me. "You two just visit together and let her knit. I'll catch the hen and chop her head off up there in the woods above the garden. Just keep busy talking, and she'll never notice. I'll pluck it, dress it, cut it up, and it will be all ready for you to fry."

I rejoined Mother, and we trekked past the garden and down the stone steps that led to the back door. We scraped our feet, went indoors, and washed our hands carefully: I at the kitchen sink; she, more properly, in the tiny round sink in the bathroom. We did the household chores, chattering like two companionable wrens. Then we dragged two small rockers from the living room out onto the little concrete terrace. Mother brought out her knitting, and we settled in to catch up on all the family news. Louise had just presented Mother with her first grandchild, and Mother showed me the pink baby blanket she was knitting for little Nancy. It was wonderful to be with Mother again and to hear about all the world I had left not so long ago.

I didn't want her to worry about our subsistence lifestyle or grieve over our isolation. I reassured her again, "We have a good time, stay very busy, and are getting to know people in the community. Farming is hard work but so much fun."

Mother smiled patiently and said, "I know you love it, dear."

"I'm sorry Barbara couldn't come with you this time. I guess she had to save her vacation days for your trip to Bermuda this summer," I offered politely.

"Yes, we're really looking forward to it. We've wanted for a long time to see Bermuda and the Caribbean area. This will be a dream vacation for both of us."

So it went as we exchanged news of our separate lives, once so close. Sandy, her glossy auburn coat contrasting with the dusty concrete of the porch, stretched out at my feet and slept peacefully. She raised her head ever so slightly and cocked her right ear. Suddenly I heard it too, a muffled cluck and then a sharp thud. I looked at Mother. She was safely engrossed in knitting the beautiful baby blanket.

Nervously I opened my mouth to continue our conversation but words failed me. Sandy left the porch in a flying leap, barking wildly. We both looked up. Wild squawks bombarded the air from the woods above the house out of our sight. We jumped to our feet and peered around the corner of the porch. The sight that greeted us was unbelievable. Hopping down the steep stone steps was our dinner, fully feathered but completely headless. Flapping her wings frantically, she took one step at a time upright. We watched in amazement, disbelieving this horror. Monroe, axe still in hand, followed, shamefaced, trying sheepishly to capture the errant bird. "I'm so sorry," he apologized. "She just got away from me." What could we do but look at each other and laugh. Monroe reclaimed his prize and went off to finish the job of getting dinner ready to cook. I restored my surprised mother to her equilibrium and rejoiced that her sense of humor outweighed her sense of propriety.

Mother stayed through her week and we all enjoyed her visit. She and I went shopping for groceries in Murphy. She wanted to smoke a cigarette as we walked around the square, but I told her that many people thought that only prostitutes smoked on the street and that real ladies chose to smoke alone at home.

There were other differences that surprised her, but she took them in good stride. Mother liked to have a drink before dinner at night, so she brought a good bottle of whiskey for the visit. We were enjoying a small drink in the living room when one of our good Baptist neighbors came walking up the driveway. "Quick, Mother, I'll put these in the kitchen," I said snatching the glasses away out of sight. My baffled mother cooperated.

Everyone wanted to meet my mother from New York. They asked her polite questions about her trip down. When she told them how long it took everyone was impressed by her kindness in coming all this way to see us. Mother was especially surprised by Rufus Vick's visit; she didn't understand why he called me by my first name, while I referred to him as Mr. Vick. As I got to know him better, I began calling him Vick, as all his friends did.

Mother seemed relieved to visit the Folk School, where she was more at ease than she was in my new farm world. Having relaxed, she enjoyed shopping for souvenirs and bought a few small carvings to take back with her as gifts. We stopped at Quedor's store in Brasstown for bread, and I introduced her to everyone there. I think that the country manners of folks there really impressed her so much that when she was ready to go home, she was more reconciled to my farm life. Mother was my regular spring visitor during the many years when I couldn't visit her in New York.

As we were getting settled into the routines of farming, Mama Wilson also came to check us out. She soon was busy helping me with whatever I undertook. She loved to walk in the woods and pick up the dry sticks that made such good kindling for our wood stove. That was helpful because the stove also provided the hot water supply for the bathtub that my mother had sent down from New York after her visit.

Monroe and I had begun clearing the hill back of the house for pasture. There were a few scattered trees and many rocks on the land. We also had started going to Green Cove Methodist Church just up the road from our place. The congregation was expanding the building and adding a rock facade. After Mama Wilson and I picked up a small truckload of rocks, Monroe delivered them to the church. Then the rock masons covered the left front corner of the building with our rocks. It always made me feel as though I were part of that church.

As the hay ripened and was cut, Monroe needed help in putting it in the barn. He turned to a common farming solution and found teenage boys who were glad to get out of school early, work some, and earn a little money. There were a few other families farming in the community, and, in exchange for Monroe's help when they had needed a crew to work, they gladly helped him with the hay. Whenever that was the case, my job was expected to fix dinner for everyone in the middle of the day.

The cherry table in our little dining room was circled with ladder-back chairs and loaded with food when the men and boys came trooping in from the fields. It was a somewhat awesome task to know how much food to prepare, but I solved it by preparing one dish for each person who would be eating with us. There was usually fried chicken or sausage, mashed potatoes, pinto beans, fresh turnip or mustard greens, a large layer cake, and probably a pudding or applesauce. Everyone was hungry and appreciative, and I loved feeling like part of the crew. Sometimes after dinner I would help throw the loose hay back into the barn loft. I remember being asked where I had learned to pitch hay. I told them that it was just like any team sport, and I had always enjoyed being part of a team.

As a wonderful bonus to our farm activities, Bernice Stalcup, Bill and Jerry's mother, became my good friend. Her husband usually spent part of each year working in Ohio where wages were many times higher and work more plentiful than in the mountains. Bernice and her children managed well until he returned. On winter evenings they often came down to play canasta with us at a card table in front of our fire in the living room.

As summer evenings lengthened and temperatures warmed, the Stalcups went swimming and often called and offered to pick me up in their open Jeep. We drove down to Hiwassee Lake below Murphy where they had found a swimming hole that was shallow and relatively safe. They were all learning to swim. I was glad to go along. Though I could never have been a lifeguard, I had been able to swim ever since I was old enough to hold my father's hand and jump the waves in the Atlantic Ocean off Long Island. I could show all the Stalcups basic swim strokes and cheer them on, and for me it was a pleasant outing.

The summer went by peacefully. In June Philip Merrill came down from New York for the Folk School's Short Course. He had been the best man at our wedding, and it was always good to see him. As soon as he arrived in Brasstown, he walked over to see us and our farm. He was full of enthusiasm for our endeavors—especially the homegrown vegetables and Sandy. We went with Philip to the folk dancing on Friday nights, a rare treat in our busy new life. He gave us a long-term subscription to *Life* and for years helped us to stay in touch with the world beyond farming. He was a supper guest who enjoyed potluck and ate fresh vegetables with such gusto that we felt like millionaires!

I really liked gardening, both flowers and vegetables. I planted flowers on the steep bank at the back of the house where Monroe and I had built a rock wall in our spare evenings. In the vegetable garden, I planted some of almost everything, and Monroe planted four rows of potatoes. We had fresh vegetables all summer; I canned the surplus for the winter. The shelves in the basement were lined with glass jars of peas, beans, corn, squash, applesauce, peaches, and a variety of greens, as well as enough jars of jelly and jam for the year.

With Velma's encouragement, I entered an exhibit at the Clay County Agricultural Fair that fall. She advised me to include weavings and other craft work that both Monroe and I had done in our years at the Folk School. We included a small table and chair and some iron candlesticks Monroe had made; my place mats and a long colorful wool runner; both fresh and canned vegetables; and jars of jams, jelly, and pickles. Everything was arranged with a pumpkin and some stalks of corn for an autumn theme. We were proud to see all we had done and even prouder to win first prize.

FOR EVERYTHING
THERE IS A SEASON

In October 1949, Monroe and I celebrated our fourth wedding anniversary. We were settled in our own house enjoying all the things we had made for it while we were at the Folk School and were planing to continue making whatever we might need in the future. We had established a working farm life and a sense of community in Brasstown. We were looking forward to the first Christmas in our own home.

We both wanted children and couldn't understand why they weren't coming along. I had consulted with Dr. Bryan Whitfield in Murphy and then visited a specialist in New York to make sure I had no physical problems. I didn't get pregnant no matter how much we enjoyed trying. Monroe was concerned enough to consult with a doctor as well. Everyone said patience was the only answer. We were told that babies often arrive with the buying of a new home. Our own new home and patience had not been enough. We were discouraged and a bit depressed.

The Christmas season at the Folk School was always fun and this year was no exception. Our good friend Philip Merrill came to play the piano, the accordion, and other instruments for the folk dancing. Other friends from New York and Washington and from various parts of the mountains came to celebrate, sing carols, and dance. The Ritchie sisters came from Kentucky and harmonized carols from an older time in the mountains, then we all sang the carols we had known from childhood.

Monroe and I went over to the school for as many of the festivities as we could fit into our farm schedule. One Saturday I joined the wreath making and decorating at the school. Afterward Monroe helped me make more wreaths and garlands for our home. We asked everyone we knew to drop by and celebrate with us as they had time. I baked all kinds of cookies and invited Bernice Stalcup to join me in decorating the cut-out sugar cookies so she could take some to her children's classes at Ogden School.

With the New Year, changes came to Brasstown. The farmers who belonged to the Mountain Valley Cooperative and sold their milk to be pasteurized and bottled in Brasstown were called to a meeting and told that the co-op had been sold to Coble Dairy. The feed and seed division of the cooperative moved to Murphy with its manager, Wayne Holland, and became Wayne's Feed and Seed, a thriving business to this day. These changes were big news for Brasstown, but for Monroe and me, the biggest news was that we were expecting a baby!

Marguerite and Georg Bidstrup were at last building their new house on the mountain land Georg had bought twenty years earlier. He had planted it in white pine seedlings that grew tall on most of the hills, but there was a clear ridgetop for the homeplace. From there you could see Brasstown Creek and the distant mountains to the west. Frank Hogan, a former student at the school who lived up on Little Brasstown Creek, was in charge of the building process; other Folk School students in the community helped.

As soon as Marguerite settled into her new house, she extended hospitality to many people, near and far. She regularly invited all the student couples in the community to come for a coffee klatch— Danish cookies, ice cream, and conversation about plans for the community. Monroe and I enjoyed being part of this group and were usually able to go. The couples with small children found it more difficult to attend, and we were looking forward to being in the same predicament.

Farming was as time-consuming as always and was going smoothly. We continued to attend Green Cove Methodist Church regularly. I particularly enjoyed Sunday school because we usually discussed the lesson as it applied to our own community. I had believed strongly for a long time that *genuine* Christianity was *applied*

Christianity, so I added my bit to the discussions. I remember one practical neighbor who brought the discussion to a close with the warning that we should all wait until after the impending election to see how far our dreams for the community could go. It was instructive for me to see that differences in political affiliation can influence one's position on Christian action.

Methodist churches in Clay County had services and preaching on a rotating basis. The ministers were usually recent graduates from Emory University in Atlanta, and we enjoyed the services led by newly ordained young ministers. They often came just for the weekend and needed a place to stay. Once we were lucky enough to host such a minister and his wife at our house. We had some wonderful discussions in front of our glowing fireplace. Even when they were called by the Methodist Church to a Clay County church, the young ministers rarely stayed more than a year. Small country congregations simply could not afford a full-time minister. A women's society met at Hickory Stand Methodist Church once a month. I attended faithfully and remember especially the programs on Christian responsibility offered by one minister's wife.

Many Sundays after church we went down to Hemp, ate dinner with Mama Wilson, and came home in time to milk the cows. On other weekends, I baked a layer cake to have on hand in case we had company. Monroe's sisters from the Copperhill—McCaysville area came most often because they lived in town and did not have farm chores and animals to tend. Of course we returned their visits and became especially close to Monroe's sister Jerry.

There were few telephones in country homes and I missed that contact with the rest of the world. When the telephone company that served Murphy had a meeting to solicit customers in Brasstown, we attended and signed up for a party-line telephone. The party-line system served twelve households and used different rings in variations of short and long buzzes to indicate which home was being called. We only heard rings for half the calls and could hear five other parties on our half of the line just as they could hear our conversations on theirs. It was polite to make a call only when our half of the line was not busy, but there was no assurance of privacy.

When I told a friend that I never listened to other people's phone conversations, she was surprised. "Aren't you interested in your neighbors?" she exclaimed. I really didn't know how to tell her that I was interested but respected the privacy of others. Such comments reminded me that I was still "from away." Despite the lack of privacy, it was great to have a telephone.

Life was good. We loved farming and worked together all day every day. We were looking forward to having a baby, and I loved being pregnant. My thin face and bony frame filled out in softer curves, and I felt wonderful. Months went by. For my thirtieth birthday in May, Mother sent me maternity dresses from New York. Then she shipped the low-sided wooden crib that had been mine. I ordered baby nightgowns, receiving blankets, and birds-eye diapers from the Sears, Roebuck catalog. I prepared one corner of our bedroom as a nursery with the baby bed and a changing table. In August the Brasstown Home Demonstration Club gave me a baby shower.

We were happier than we had ever been. The baby was active, jumping and kicking vigorously within me. We were so excited and thankful. One day as I was wielding the broom over the hardwood floor near the front door, the baby gave a sudden and violent lurch. I clutched my swollen stomach and all was still.

That night in bed I confided to Monroe that the baby was very calm. "See if you can feel him kick," I begged. He laid his hand on my stomach and said reassuringly. "The little fellow is just resting. Go to sleep."

Later that week I went for my regular visit with Dr. Whitfield and told him about the experience. He examined me with the stethoscope. Inadvertently, with disappointment, frustration, and shock, he exclaimed under his breath, "There's no heartbeat." When I dressed and went into his office, he was more reassuring. "Perhaps the baby is turned away so that I can't hear a heartbeat. We'll x-ray next week and see what we can find. I don't want to use the x-ray unless I have to. You continue to take care of yourself. You have done nothing wrong. I'll see you Tuesday."

Dr. Whitfield's office was at the back of the first floor of the Murphy General Hospital. I stumbled out of his office, down the

long, dark hallway to the front door, then down the steep stone steps
to the sidewalk on Peachtree Street. Monroe had gone to do errands,
and I was to meet him downtown. Tears streaming down my cheeks, I
staggered two blocks to the middle of town, numb to all surroundings.
The street was a shambles. Construction was underway in front of
the new A&P grocery store next door to the old First Baptist Church.
Monroe was parked there with the red truck and I climbed in. I don't
know what we said to each other. I was just thankful to find him and
to be able to go home. I'm sure he knew how desperate I felt.

In spite of despair, we hoped for a miracle. Next week the x-ray
showed a perfectly formed baby boy, but still no heartbeat could be
detected. Dr. Whitfield cautioned us to wait, saying reassuringly that
the apple will drop when it is ready. "For the sake of future pregnan-
cies it is better to go for natural childbirth rather than have a Caesar-
ean to deliver the child," he advised in his kind, old-fashioned style.

Wait, we did. I couldn't bear the thought of sympathy, so we
told no one. As I sat in the hallway outside Dr. Whitfield's office one
morning waiting for my weekly appointment, I overheard a nurse
and a secretary in the front office regretting my loss with deep sympathy. "She wanted this baby so much."

My denial was strong enough and faith true enough to still hope
for a miracle, so we kept to ourselves. Weeks went by. Monroe hired
two friends to help him clear the cut-over woodlot at the far side of
the big cornfield next to the woods. I walked out there twice a day to
carry them water or coffee for midmorning or afternoon breaks, and
then I cooked a hearty farmhands' dinner for them at noon. I was
rewarded with their respect and gentle appreciation.

The doctor said he would induce labor when the time comes. I
called my mother to tell her that the baby was dead, but I would be
fine. She was shocked, but only concerned for me, not for the loss
that was breaking my heart. As Monroe sat beside me and listened
to me talk, tears streamed down his cheeks, the only time I ever saw
him cry.

I had read everything I could find about natural childbirth,
determined I would deliver my baby this way. My distress did not
change my mind. On was the first day of autumn, September 21,

1950, Dr. Whitfield induced labor by rupturing the amnionic sac. I was fully conscious and heard him say clearly, "Oh, that damned cord, wrapped around and around his neck."

The attending nurses were surprised at my objectivity as I commented when he finished the delivery, "It went just like the book said it would." I had already done much of my grieving. Dr. Whitfield talked to me, giving me comforting recommendations. He advised that I not ask to see the baby who was so small that it would just increase my grief. I told him we planned to name our son after Monroe and he would be buried in the family cemetery at Hemp, Georgia. Dr. Whitfield advised that I would need to stay in the hospital for a few days and should miss that ceremony.

Now that the ordeal was over, I tried to put my grief behind me as I lay alone in a narrow hospital bed in Murphy General Hospital. Darkness gathered outside as the busy activity of caregivers and patients slowed within the building. On the street, businesses closed, workers went home for the night, and traffic came almost to a standstill.

Monroe came to visit with me as I picked at the supper on my tray, delivered by a kitchen worker with a cheery smile. She and the nurses were so upbeat, but their pity shone through and bothered me as I tried desperately to be brave. Monroe went alone to Georgia to tell his mother and sisters about our loss and to make arrangements for a cemetery plot and burial services. We needed to be together now, but he had work to do and I had to regain my strength.

After he left I asked to see the other mother and her baby in the tiny maternity wing. She came in for a visit. Gently she unwrapped the swaddling blanket and showed me her baby's tiny fingers and toes, the perfection of a healthy, newborn life. Her kindness comforted me, and the sight and touch and sound of her child convinced me that my pregnancy and the birth of my stillborn baby were real. The doctor told me that I could have other children, so I knew that this experience had to be meaningful. But how would my son's short life within me be of any value?

I knew that Monroe had a difficult errand to accomplish that night and wished I could have gone with him. I was thankful for his faith in God. It was nurtured in him from early childhood in the Methodist church in Hemp. My own faith was also strong. Even in my deep sorrow, I was grateful for the eight months I had experienced as a mother.

SPIRITUAL GROWTH

❦

Clearly it was time to give up the intellectual questions I had about the church and mature in the faith that had sustained us both. I had been baptized as an infant. When a small child, I prayed every night with my mother and attended church with my parents. At fifteen I went to Saint Timothy's School, an excellent Episcopal preparatory boarding school to get ready for college. There we had morning and evening prayer and hymn singing with roll call every day. The Victorian regimen of behavior at the school instilled self-discipline. Classes filled me with many intellectual interests and a curiosity to learn more.

Sundays at school were devoted to worship. We attended three services in the parish church next door to the school, and I became deeply attached to the beauty of worship. We spent an hour hymn singing after breakfast and an hour in Bible study after supper! I was confirmed at that church in May 1935. The bishop's text was "Behold, I stand at the door and knock," (Revelation 3:20). In my mind this text was closely associated with the command of Jesus, "Ask, and it will be given you; seek, and you will find; knock, and it will be opened to you," (Matthew 7: 7).

In college I was an asker, a seeker, and a knocker. I visited many churches and attended daily chapel services as regularly as my schedule allowed. My study of the history of Christianity and the Church's role in social action raised many questions about the behavior of the institutional Church and its teachings. However, during the years of World War II, I sought comfort in prayer and worship wherever it was available in whatever church I chose. While I worked in New York, often during lunch hour I went into St. Patrick's Cathedral across Fifth Avenue from the Rockefeller Center. I sat quietly by myself, praying and reflecting on the Bible.

I had always asked questions and had doubts about religion, but as I lay in that hospital bed in September 1950, there was no doubt in my mind that despite intellect, doubt, and different customs, faith must be nurtured. I gave thanks to God who comforted me, and I resolved to grow spiritually through discipline, practice, and community with others.

There have been many other turning points in my life, but this was a crucial one. That lonely night in the Murphy hospital, I gave thanks for the life of my first son. I resolved that he had not lived in vain. In death he gave me the gift of faith in God's help in time of trouble, hope for the future, and a lasting joy in the miracle of life. Faith, hope, joy, and thanksgiving shaped my love for children and became focal points in my life.

As time went on, Dr. Whitfield became a good friend as well as my doctor. He and his wife, Annette, were originally from Alabama and had moved to Murphy when the doctor opened his practice there in the 1940s. The Whitfields were cradle Episcopalians and very active in the church in Murphy. Through the years of World War II, the church had received little attention from the Diocese of Western North Carolina. With staff shorthanded, the diocese had concentrated its efforts on the most populated area around Asheville during those years. The long-established Church of the Messiah in Murphy had relied on faithful Episcopalians and a temporary deacon to conduct services. They had not been visited by a bishop for several years.

With the consecration of the Reverend Matthew George Henry as bishop of the Episcopal Diocese of Western North Carolina in September 1948, the diocese came alive. Bishop Henry was only thirty-eight years old. He had been the rector of Christ Church in Charlotte. He was filled with energy and the missionary spirit, eager to form relationships with outlying churches and missions in spite of scarce financial resources and the sparse population in the mountains.

When Dr. Whitfield suggested that we come to the Church of the Messiah in Murphy when the bishop made his visit in 1950, he brought me back into the Episcopal Church. As country people, Monroe and I felt timid about going to a church in town, but we both enjoyed the service. Monroe was used to the informality of a north Georgia country Methodist church, but he really enjoyed the liturgy of the Episcopal service. Despite my criticism of the Church's neglect of the social gospel, I loved the hymns, prayers, and Communion of the Protestant Episcopal Church. I had known them all my life.

After visiting at Messiah, we continued to go to the Methodist church in our own community, but liturgy drew us back to Messiah for special occasions. Early in 1951, soon after his visitation at Messiah, Bishop Henry sent a newly ordained young priest, the Reverend Rhett Winters, to be Vicar-in-Charge at Messiah. He and his wife, who was expecting their first child soon, moved into the small rectory in Murphy. Perhaps the bishop chose Mr. Winters because he too was filled with evangelical zeal.

Mr. Winters looked through the church records and identified four couples who came sporadically to services at Messiah from neighboring Clay County. He must have been convinced that there was a need for an Episcopal Church in Clay County, because he visited each in turn, beginning with Rufus and Dot Vick and ending with Monroe and me. I was relieved to talk to a minister who was not shocked by my questions about faith and who enjoyed answering them. Mr. Winters then suggested that we start a study group in our homes in Clay County. These monthly study meetings gave us the education, fellowship, and spiritual strength to serve others as we grew into a church.

Our first study meeting was in Hayesville at the Vicks' house. Vick had recently married Dot, a music teacher from Franklin. They were attending the First Methodist Church in Hayesville, but Vick missed the Episcopal Church of his childhood. The Vicks already knew the Moores, Quentin and Ruth, who also attended First Methodist. Ruth was a cradle Episcopalian from Hastings, Nebraska, who had married Quentin Moore when he was stationed there before going overseas to Europe. The third couple was Jim and Eva Ledford. Jim was a Baptist, who had lived much of his life in Clay County, while Eva was a lifelong Episcopalian from West Virginia. This group became the nucleus of an Episcopalian congregation in Hayesville.

That June evening was a great success. The men were congenial and enjoyed telling jokes, a skill at which Monroe excelled. The women, most meeting for the first time, enjoyed learning about each other. Rhett Winters relaxed in the informal family atmosphere and, with his wife and baby, was quickly at ease in our group. The Ledfords agreed to have the next meeting at their country store on the remote, winding gravel road to Tusquittee.

Monroe and I were the last to arrive at that second meeting of our infant study group. We didn't know the Tusquittee community and missed the little store hidden in a curve as we drove up the valley. There were few houses, and we couldn't find anyone to ask for directions. As we reached the point where the road looped back toward Hayesville, we just sat and laughed at ourselves for being lost in Clay County. We debated whether to drive on home or to go back the way we had come and look more closely. Luckily that's just what we did. There, nestled in the curve of the road, was the home and country store of the Ledfords.

The Moores and the Vicks were already there, enjoying refreshments. Jim and Eva greeted us with hospitality like that of the Christians on Pentecost in the Book of Acts, where people of very different language groups were all welcomed together. Meeting in the informality of the store set us all at ease. Their children entertained us with corny jokes and tricks before they left us for bed. We all wanted families, and these two gave us assurance and hope for the future of our church family.

Ruth and Quentin Moore lived in west Hayesville. We met there most often because it was centrally located, and they had the largest living room. Quentin was a natural leader and the only person in our group who had been born in Clay County. The rest of us, coming "from away," were lonely for a familiar feeling of fellowship. There was a strong desire for an Episcopal Church in Clay County. County loyalty was always important, and we didn't want to go to church in Murphy, Cherokee County. We were an interesting collection of seekers, all interested in learning more about Christianity.

When our turn came to host the group, everyone drove to Brass-town and crowded around our fireplace, several sitting cross-legged on the floor. Rhett Winters was a good teacher and the Seabury teaching series was an excellent springboard for discussions. He helped us differentiate between the politics of church formation and the belief of individuals. Even more importantly, Mr. Winters encouraged us to be involved in learning, to enjoy fellowship together, and to ask questions. This set the stage for all of us to examine feelings, thoughts, and doubts honestly. He assured us that God accepts each of us, "faults and all."

We had so much fun together that we started having outings and potlucks in addition to our Sunday study meetings. We had picnics up on remote Tuni Gap, at picnic tables on Lake Chatuge, and in our own backyards. Our families began to grow, as did our church family. Bud and Frances Roberts and their children joined us from Sylva at a meeting in the Vick's tiny apartment in 1954. Couples from England and Australia with ties to the Anglican Church joined us at times when they were in our area.

When Mr. Winters left us for another parish, we continued to meet on Sunday afternoons. Evening Prayer services were led by Rufus Vick or Quentin Moore for several months. We saved the money we had been contributing to Mr. Winter's salary in anticipation of having another vicar.

When Bishop Henry sent another ordained minister, William Russell, to the Church of the Messiah, and to provide services to our group in Hayesville, we elected a vestry for the first time. Rufus Vick became the senior warden, Quentin Moore the treasurer, and I the clerk. We met with the vestry of Messiah and a representative of the diocese at the Hotel Regal in Murphy to discuss the details of the relationship between the two parishes, deciding that our church would be known as the Church of the Good Shepherd.

With our growing numbers—we all had children now—we found that our homes were becoming too small for services. Bishop Henry visited Good Shepherd on October 3, 1954, and confirmed our second senior warden, Quentin Moore, at his home in Hayesville. Then, in 1955, we rented the meeting room on the ground floor of the Masonic Building in Hayesville where we had church suppers on Saturday night once a month and Sunday morning services at nine o'clock each week. We arrived early to set up folding chairs and improvise a portable altar. The early hour made it possible for our shared minister to hurry back to Murphy for the service there at eleven. This was our arrangement for several years until our good treasurer saved enough money for a down payment on land, and we began to build our first all-purpose building in 1959.

CHILDREN AND DOGS

After buying our home and farm in April 1949, Monroe and I began the decade of the 1950s with high hopes for farming and a family. We had been devastated by the death of our unborn son, but we were comforted by the support of our neighbors and by the love we felt within our small group of Episcopalians in Clay County. Soon we were blessed with the successive arrival of our four children.

Danny was born in 1951. He became the center of our lives and was welcomed by our families and the community. His arrival was greeted with many gifts from our friends. The Folk School blacksmith, Oscar Cantrell, brought our son his first toy car, a red convertible that raced around the floor under our Christmas tree. Bernice's sister made him a little blue suit to wear for his baptism on Easter Sunday in Murphy. Rufus Vick was Danny's proud godfather. Everyone rejoiced that at last we had a family.

Danny was a remarkable toddler; he never met a stranger. He won everyone's heart as he took tentative steps, named everything he saw, and remembered everyone he met. He loved having company and shared his toys with any child who visited. He enjoyed it when I read to him and spent nap time trying to name all the characters in his picture books. He went with me to the chicken house, riding on my hip to gather eggs, and he learned to count to one hundred by the time he was three.

When Dan was barely four years old, the fledgling PTA at Ogden School urged me to join and help foster good relationships between parents and teachers there. The first meeting was an eye-opener for me. A large crowd of parents gathered to organize the group. In the past I had only attended PTA meetings as a student or teacher; now I was a proud parent. Those who invited me probably expected me to be a leader because of my education, and because I was "from away." Unfortunately, I have always been an essentially shy person with little self-confidence and no desire to lead. When the organizing parents called on me to speak, I said a few words and sat down.

They then asked for a volunteer to speak and lead the meeting. Several women volunteered. I wish I could remember the name of the lady who stepped forward. She rose to her feet and went to the front of the room. Without any notes, but with heartfelt words, she spoke at length about the need to support our children and to make Ogden School the very best it could be. Words did not fail her, and that day I learned that grammar was not important. Her passionate belief in the value of education and the importance of children led her on and on. It was inspiring for me to observe her self-confidence and conviction.

Fortunately I was able to wait until Danny was in school before I became the "cookie lady" for his class, and for many more classes that followed, at Ogden School. I was a faithful member of the PTA, a substitute teacher, and even the teacher of the fifth grade for one year when enrollment increased and they needed an extra teacher there. I don't think I ever became a good public speaker though.

At home there was a sandbox between the back door and the steps down from the barnyard. Monroe also built a slide and hung an old tire swing from a large tree near the garage. Danny's playmates often came over from neighboring farms. All of the boys loved to play Cowboys and Indians like the Westerns that dominated television at that time. There were toy guns scattered all over the yard, gifts of thoughtful neighbors who remembered their popularity with their own children.

On the farm, we were having lean times financially because the price of milk was falling and the price of feed rising. Small-time farming was not as independent an enterprise as I had imagined. Our farming was closely tied to big business and dependent on market fluctuations over which we had no control. Coble Dairy bought our milk and sold us chicken feed. They were always one month behind in paying for the milk, but more than prompt in charging for the feed. In the winter of 1955, we had a retroactive price decrease for the milk we had sold two months earlier. Of course, we had already paid for feed for the chickens. It definitely made finances tight, especially when our yearly payment on the farm was due.

Fortunately, Vick visited us often at the farm and we saw him on Sundays at church, so he was able to advise us. He told us that the county farm office secretary was going on maternity leave and asked me if I could type. I told him that I had hunted and pecked my way through college, typing papers for fellow students at ten cents a page (eleven for a carbon-copy version). He offered me the office job for the duration of the secretary's leave.

My primary task would be to type up reports given to me by the four agents: Vick and Velma, Hank Rosenkrantz, and a young assistant home agent. Monroe thought that he and Danny, who was just four, could manage without me. It was autumn and time to gather corn. Danny could ride on the load and keep his daddy company. So I went to work in the county office, leaving them together to gather the fields of corn.

I typed so slowly that I had to work through my lunch hour most days, and I was often still hunting and pecking out the weekly reports for the state office when the staff went home at five o'clock. The agents were patient, but their handwriting was often hard to decipher, and I had to read it slowly and carefully. Velma suggested that they could just tell me what they had accomplished during the week. Then I could compose the weekly reports for each agent to read, correct, and sign each Friday.

I knew the agents, their weekly routines, and the farms they visited, so writing the reports myself made matters at work much easier for us all. It freed the agents from having to compose their remarks, and it was easier for me to write their reports than to read their hurried scrawl. It left me time to do other clerical jobs like making copies of recipes or other information to distribute to the farm families. For the short time I worked at the county farm office, I loved the friendliness of the agents, the occasional lunch group at

Booth's drugstore, and the weekly paycheck that helped make our yearly farm payment possible.

Soon after Danny's fourth birthday, Anne was born, a beautiful petite baby with a strong will and little need to sleep or eat! She had difficulty nursing and we had trouble finding a formula that agreed with her. At three months she weighed only nine pounds. We gradually switched her from formula to cultured buttermilk on which she thrived.

Naps were a different matter. She was never sleepy. At first she liked her basket and lay contentedly watching a swinging toy. Sometimes she tried shaking her rattle. At night I pulled the basket close to my side of the bed and jiggled it gently until she dozed off, repeating as necessary whenever she woke. As she grew older, I rocked her after lunch until she fell asleep and then gently carried her to her crib. It was a challenge. Anything could go wrong with the routine. An airplane flying over the house would rouse her. Our neighbor's lawn mower in action erased all hope of peace. But Anne grew, flourished, walked, or ran to explore everything in the house.

To supplement the income from the farm, Monroe accepted a job at a small manufacturing plant halfway up Old Route 64 toward Warne. Gustave Lidseen, Inc., made stainless steel baking pans and pipe-bending devices. Monroe worked there several years and was in charge of the shipping department. However, before he started work we planted a three-acre field with red peppers to sell to the Campbell Soup Company's canning factory in Blairsville, Georgia.

The peppers grew well and produced a bumper crop, and by September the field was full of green peppers beginning to turn red. It was time to harvest. Monroe left home early each morning and came back at supper time. So Danny and Anne and I went to work in the pepper field right after we ate lunch together. Contented to watch, Anne lay on a quilt near the edge of the field, shaded by our prize apple tree. Danny and I each carried an old feed sack and started at the top of a row of peppers and picked the red ones, dropping them into the sacks we pulled behind us. We walked down the rows abreast, gradually filled each sack, then took them to the side of the field where we poured the peppers into the back of the pickup truck parked near Anne's apple tree.

The first day we covered the bottom of the truck bed. It was slow going, but we did feel a sense of accomplishment. Danny was a valiant worker, and Anne took a long nap in the open air. The next day Mama Wilson came up from Georgia to babysit with Anne while we worked. That was a big help, but picking was tedious and surprisingly hard work. Anne always had a mind of her own, preferred me, and was difficult for Mama Wilson to quiet.

When we had picked all of the peppers that were ripe and had a full load, Grandma went home. After both children were in bed, Monroe and I prepared the crop ready for me to take it to Blairsville. The next morning after Monroe left for work, I hung Anne's car seat in the middle of the front seat in the truck. I gave Danny her bottle and pacifier to hold for her if she became restless, and we set off.

It was perhaps thirty miles down to Blairsville. The pepper-collection plant was in a large, open storage building right across from the elementary school. Danny was delighted. After we checked in, he got out of the truck to watch the children on the playground. Then it was time to pull the truck up and have our peppers weighed and graded, another process he enjoyed watching. Anne was happy to be out of her car seat and nestled in my arms where she could see people and they could ooh and aah at her. By eleven in the morning we had completed the whole process and were ready to drive home—three tired, contented people. I don't know how many similar trips we made that fall, but enough. On weekends Monroe did the largest part of the work of gathering and sorting. That left the children and me with only Mondays to travel and ample time during the week to make many jars of sweet red pepper relish.

After the harvest and getting our check for the pepper crop, I breathed a deep sign of relief. Then I silently reassessed my abilities to care for the family of four children of which I had always dreamed. Maybe I wouldn't be able to do all that would be needed for such a large family. Maybe Monroe and I couldn't give them a good life.

The doubts soon faded. It was too late to turn back. We were thankful that I was pregnant again. I had always wanted children, and we welcomed all the children we could possibly have into our family. John arrived in July and was the easiest, most agreeable infant anyone could ever imagine. He was no trouble at all—a most contented baby, who held his own bottle early and put himself to sleep without any rocking.

Danny started to school at Ogden. He walked down the driveway and rode the school bus. He was thankful that his friend, Eston Stalcup, protected him from the teasing of the older children on the school bus. He liked school and the stories they read in their primers. He often simplified the text with understanding instead of reading the words literally. For instance, the word *mother* he often read as *mama*. He was also proud of learning to write and practiced faithfully.

I think Anne felt lonely because her brother was at school through the week. She was just of the right age to hold crayons and color in her picture books. She often knew no limits, and she had a love of color. The walls in the hallway made good canvases, and Danny's homework papers were often decorated, much to his dismay. However, from that early beginning, we realized that Anne would be the artist in the family.

Two years later on a Sunday evening in 1959, my neighbor, Blanche Smith, came up through the woods that adjoined our houses to visit a while. We had been picnicking all afternoon on the edge of Lake Chatuge and my feet were covered in the red mud I had waded through as I watched the children swim. Blanche and I talked in a leisurely way, and then I told her I needed to run a bath and wash my feet. The telephone rang before I could get into the water. It was my sister Barbara calling to tell me that Mother was in the hospital having had a heart attack. As she talked, I went into labor with child number four. Barbara assured me that I didn't have to worry about Mother, but I caught my breath, calmed down, and managed to say good-bye.

Suddenly our leisurely day had to shift into high gear. I didn't even have time to wash my muddy feet in the tub. Monroe called Jerry to come and stay with the children. Another neighbor arrived to drive me to the hospital in Murphy, and to our surprise and delight our bouncy daughter, Florence, arrived even before the doctor. She had a full head of dark red hair. Happily, Mother recovered just fine.

Our children were just what I wanted—a family of delightfully distinct personalities. I took them everywhere I needed to go. People admired them and repeatedly commented on how different they all were: two with beautiful big, brown eyes, two with blue; a dark, curly head, two towheads, and a redhead.

We all went shopping in Murphy at the A&P grocery store and at the dime store on Main Street. As they grew, we went to the swimming pool and the children's playground in Murphy. I will never forget the lady who supervised the children's playground. She was watchful, careful, and very kind. She often included Danny with the younger children so that I was free to do some errands alone. After everything else was done we usually went to the public library and selected a high stack of new books to take home with us. Finally, our last stop was Mrs. Arrant's Ice Cream Parlor. The reward for good behavior was an ice cream cone to eat as we drove home.

On Sundays we all went to church in the new building our Episcopal congregation built and moved into before Easter in 1959. We always sat in our own second-row pew for the service. Florence was the first baby to be baptized at Good Shepard. It was so cold in October without any heat in the block building that Florence turned blue, and we all shivered through the service. Soon thereafter, our eldest member, Mrs. Meyer, who had retired from New Jersey, donated our first oil heater, becoming a sort of fairy godmother to us all.

Danny enjoyed being a Cub Scout, loved his uniform, and looked forward to each camping trip. A tragic accident took one of his fellow Cub Scouts, and the den was asked to be present at the funeral. Monroe and Danny went to the ceremony in an old-time fundamentalist church, where the preacher took the opportunity to "scare the hell" out of the boys. His colorful visions of punishment from a judgmental God had the effect of giving Danny nightmares. For months after that he walked in his sleep. After going to bed peacefully, he would get up and try to get out of the house. The tragic Cub Scout funeral experience firmly convinced us again that we wanted our children to grow up knowing and loving a just and beneficent

God. We were thankful for the Church of the Good Shepherd and continued to pile into our red truck and go there each Sunday.

We eventually sold our dairy herd, keeping one cow to supply us with milk. I could hardly bear to see my calves and young heifers go to another farm. We often drove up to the road outside their pasture fence so I could watch the pretty heifers I had hand fed grow from wobbly calves to healthy heifers ready to calve and give milk.

Our red truck was definitely showing its mileage. The floor in the cab was so worn that we could see the road passing under our feet. Six of us filled it tightly, but we didn't feel safe allowing the children to ride in the bed of the truck for any distance on the bumpy roads. So, in 1963, we sold it and bought a new, shiny black station wagon.

We decided it was our turn to go visit Grandma Lambert and Aunt Barbara The children really needed to see the city, so our first trip in the new station wagon was to New York. We were shy about traffic and so planned to use the Blue Ridge Parkway to travel through Virginia. We found a motel to spend the first night. Later the children always remembered the motel with the red door where there were other children to play with before supper.

We drove into New York City on Friday night as the weekend traffic was coming out. We checked into a hotel and took a taxi to visit Mother and my sister Barbara, who now lived together in New York City. We saw Rockefeller Center and St. Patrick's Cathedral and rode on the top level of the Fifth Avenue buses to do our city sightseeing. Danny celebrated his twelfth birthday there. With a sigh of relief, we drove out of the city on Sunday evening before the city dwellers returned. The drive home included a short visit to the beach in North Carolina and a long trip home.

Later that summer on beautiful hot afternoons, I often filled our station wagon with children from our congregation and took every-one to "The Point"at Lake Chatuge to swim. Ruth Moore and her son, Alan, were usually among the crowd, and the Roberts children and others also came regularly. After my childhood acquaintance with the Atlantic Ocean and the icy waters of northern Maine, I finally became used to the soupy water of the lake. It was a great way to cool off, and everyone in that group learned to swim.

When there were no extra children ready to go with us, we sometimes took our faithful dog who was always a water lover. Even if it was too cold or rainy for us, the dog never tired of swimming after sticks thrown out into the lake.

We actually had a succession of four-legged friends, all swimmers. Our copper-colored cocker spaniel, Sandy, who was pregnant when we moved to the farm. She had been an outdoor dog, but after losing Chipsie, we were cautious and kept Sandy inside most of the time. Monroe fenced in a small dog kennel and lot on the edge of the woods above the house. We thought it was appropriate for a maternity ward, but Sandy got into trouble after delivering her first pup. We had to call the vet to deliver four more, but they did not live.

We felt sorry for Sandy and the pup and moved them into the living room. With our next litter, we kept Cruiser and Freckles and sold the rest as soon as they were six weeks old. Our plan to raise and sell puppies was abandoned after one of our buyers told us that her puppy was such a nuisance that she "just put her out in the gap of the mountain." We couldn't bear to think of such cruelty to our baby dog. We stopped raising puppies, but new dogs chose us.

Perhaps the first pet to choose us was a bedraggled little dog who lived in downtown Brasstown. We felt sorry for her when her family moved away and left her. We adopted her and named her Molly. Soon she had puppies. We found good homes for each of them but kept Molly all her life. All the dogs were free to run in and out of the house, but usually stayed close. All sorts of dogs joined our family and were loved and lost during our farm years.

When Anne was in the third grade at Ogden School, she wrote a letter at school on lined notebook paper:

"Dear Santa Claus, I have been a good girl all year. We live on a farm. I want my own puppy for Christmas. Please bring me one. Love, Anne."

When she came home that afternoon, she told us about it. She twisted one strand of golden brown hair around her left forefinger, twirled it, and closed her big brown eyes to think. "I wonder if Mrs. May will mail our letters," she mused. "Do you think there really is a Santa Claus?" Though Anne didn't say any more about it, she apparently had doubts about whether Santa would bring her puppy, picturing in the back of her head a beautiful curly, white poodle she would name Fifi. She told me she was glad she had written a neat letter. She described the tricks she would teach Fifi. She dreamed on, imagining clearly how Fifi would look and how she would take care of her own little puppy.

Christmas morning came. Anne woke up before daylight, her heart beating quickly in anticipation. Maybe Fifi was sitting under the tree. She slipped out of bed and tiptoed to the living room. Pushing open the door just a crack, she surveyed the living room in the gray light. No puppy waiting there. She went disconsolately back to bed to wait for the rest of the family to get up. Finally the others were crowding ahead of her down the hall. "We'll open our stockings first, see what Santa left for us," Dad called, "before we open the presents under the tree."

Fifi hadn't appeared under the tree. Anne was so disappointed that she hardly had the heart to see what Santa had put in her stocking. Slowly she extracted one thing after another: a small mirror, Hershey kisses, a tangerine, some good smelling soap, a pink lip balm almost as good as lipstick. Then, curled at the very bottom of her stocking, there was a bright red dog collar with a printed note attached, "I'm waiting for you in the barn. Come and get me!" Anne stood up quickly, spilling her stocking treasures out of her lap. Dad was watching. "Put on your coat and cap and mittens. We'll go up there as soon as you're ready. The others can go on opening presents."

No need to urge her. As ready as a new battery, Anne pranced up to the barn with Dad; her hand in his kept her from soaring right off the ground. As they reached the feed room door on the side of the big barn, they heard a sharp "Yip, yip," then a wild scratching against the door. Dad turned the knob, opened the door, and there was the puppy: black and white and tan, long white-tipped tail thumping wildly, and a pleading whine welcoming release.

"Merry Christmas, Anne, she's yours."

"But . . . but, what is it?"

"She's a purebred beagle, all yours. Santa Claus brought her for you. Aren't you surprised?"

Surprised in a way her dad couldn't imagine! Anne sat down on ground as cold as her heart and crossed her arms over her chest. Oblivious to the rebuff, the pup jumped into her lap and curled her plump, warm body into Anne's triangle of crossed legs and laid her head on Anne's red-flanneled knee. With eyes as big and brown as Anne's and wiggling from head to toe, she licked the reluctant receiver's face. Slowly Anne smiled. "I thought . . ." The lump in Anne's throat melted as the pup snuggled as a ball in her lap. Anne looked up at her Dad's questioning face. "She wants me to love her, doesn't she, Dad?"

"Yes. What will you name her?"

"Poochie." No fluffy white poodle for her. Fifi was gone forever. This was her puppy, a beautiful tri-colored beagle, Anne's own.

Danny and a friend invested in a tall pup that was half Doberman Pinscher and half German shepherd. They thought he would make an excellent watchdog, and they could sell him for big money. It was a good joke. Silas looked fierce, but he was the gentle, loving friend of all. At first, people who drove up were so afraid of his fierce appearance that they wouldn't get out of the car and come to the house, but he hardly even barked at strangers. Silas became my good friend and guide and met me in the garage whenever I came home late at night. His head was at my waist level, and I could rest my hand on his head and walk fearlessly to the house.

Silas, Poochie, Molly, and a fourth dog we called Noname formed a squirrel-hunting team in the backyard. They chased any squirrel traveling through the trees overhead. Poochie spotted the squirrel, pointed and barked sharply; Silas ran after it first, as fast as the squirrel traveled; while Poochie barked on, running swiftly; Molly followed; and last came Noname who never gave up the chase until the squirrel was long out of sight through the woods and over the hill. There is no way of ever fully expressing our love and appreciation for our dogs over the years—we remember them with heartfelt thanks.

As the children in the neighborhood went through Ogden School, they were joined at play and adventure on our farm on many Saturdays by Martin and Loren Ramsey, whose father had recently become the director of the Folk School. One memorable Saturday, an event occurred that would become a Wilson family legend—a story that was told and retold so many times, I feel I observed every detail.

"The Ramsays are here, and we're going to build a house in the woods. Come on if you want to help," John called to his sisters as he let the screen door slam behind him. "Tommy and Terry are already waiting for us up at the barn."

Florence followed close behind, and they greeted Martin and Loren who had inveigled a ride from their home at the Folk School. Anne led a raid on the supply of rakes in the garage and warned the others, "We'd better get out of sight before Mom thinks of something more for us to do!"

The Saturday October sky was a bright Carolina blue, the clouds pure white. The trees had deposited most of their brilliant leaves on the floor of the forest. It hadn't rained in several weeks. Over the hill from the house there were stands of mixed hardwoods. The children shuffled through the thick undercoating of leaves in a game of catch-up-follow-the-leader. Zigzagging over ancient fallen trees, jumping over rocks in a convoluted journey, the gang arrived at a cleared spot on the promontory jutting out over Old Route 64.

The previous winter Monroe had cut some trees there to saw into lumber for a new shed on the barn. After sending the logs to the sawmill, Monroe and the boys had cut the larger branches into short pieces for the fireplace. The smaller branches were left to dry out. "This is the spot," John said. "This is the flat place we found last week. There are enough big limbs for the framework and dried pine branches to cover them."

Martin had been scouting the farther perimeter. "I can see our house at the Folk School from here," he called.

"We need to clear all the little twigs off and sweep the floor space clean," Loren suggested.

Terry fell into the role of foreman easily because his father did construction work. The others respected his bossiness. "Well, boys, let's get to work. After we clear this spot, we'll take these biggest branches and lean them up against each other. John, you get that one that's the size of this one and we'll meet in the middle. The rest of you do the same in a circle so that they're all leaning toward each other. That'll be the framework, and we'll pile the brush on top."

"It will be just like an Indian teepee," Loren observed. "They knew how to live in the woods."

For a while they were busy constructing the framework and sweeping the floor clean. "We need to leave some doors," John directed.

"And some windows, if we can," Florence added.

Over the next half hour, the house in the woods took shape. There was a wide entrance and two small back doors. The sweet-smelling branches of dried pine covered the framework, making a cozy dark interior. Terry placed rocks in the center of the floor in a small circle.

"What's that for?" Loren asked.

"The fireplace. We need one to pow-wow around. The smoke can go up through the hole where the branches come together in the middle. Let's pile some more pine around the sides for beds."

For a while they worked on. The house had taken shape and they gathered inside. Terry began piling twigs in the fireplace. He reached deep in his pocket for matches. There were murmurs but no outright argument.

"The smoke will go right up through that hole," Terry said again. There were a few moments of satisfaction as they savored their hideaway and the excitement of sitting around their campfire. Martin began telling a story he had heard about the Cherokees. Then suddenly—panic!

"It's spreading. Hurry! Put it out. The framework is catching fire." They beat at the fire in the circle of rocks, but the fire spread outward and upward. "We'd better get out. It's burning up. Quick, quick!" Everyone scurried for a door and stood watching in horror as the flames reached up and out through the brush.

Everyone was talking at once: "We need help . . . The woods will catch; there'll be a forest fire . . . Martin, run down to the road and stop anyone who's passing . . . Terry, run for the store and get help there . . . Florence, run to the house and get Mom . . . I'll get some buckets and water at the barn . . . Loren, you and Tommy stay here and beat it out with the extra branches . . . Let's rake a clearing around it if we can."

They all ran in different directions, leaving Loren and Tommy to try to keep it from spreading. Martin found help on the highway. Terry recruited men at the store, and they called the Folk School for help. Florence alerted Mom, and Anne went in search of Dad. John carried two buckets of water from the barn spigot. Everyone else took gallon jugs from the house.

For a while it looked as though all the woods would go up in smoke. Then as men came from all directions, the fire was contained. By lunchtime the seven exhausted builders stood shamefaced around the white ashes of their house in the woods.

"I thought we had to hurry and get out here to build it," John observed," but I never knew before what hurry really is, or what many hands can do."

"No one who came to help even told us what a dumb idea that was," Terry observed. "What'll we do next week?"

It was a great time in our lives on the farm. There was always a variety of things to do, animals to love and care for, work to be done, softball games in the farm fields, trees to climb, mischief to risk. Fortunately the brush burning was the only serious misadventure we experienced in those years of fun on the farm.

Once John climbed too high in a tree with brittle branches in the woods and fell to the ground. He was afraid he had broken his back and lay still until his calls for help brought Dad to set him back on his feet. In later years Anne confessed that she often sneaked off to the store to get refreshments, posting Florence to watch and warn of parents' discovery.

In addition to all that went on at home and school, there was always interaction with the Folk School. In the summer there was Little Folk School instead of summer camp for all the community children. It left plenty of time for them to help with farming at home and for occasional trips to the beach or special school programs. Danny's first job away from home was milking cows in the Folk School barn.

We all made accessories for our home throughout the year and, of course, Christmas presents to send away. Our sewing, cooking, weaving, embroidery, carving, stenciling, and woodworking were greatly influenced by the creativity of the Folk School. Moreover, we were always enriched by friendships with the people "from away" who came and went for summer Short Courses.

Our children also loved the Friday Night dancing at the Folk School. Everyone learned to do the English Country "long ways," Danish folk dances, the jig, and the waltz. Folk dancing was wonderful recreation and kept us in close touch with the Folk School.

Florence participated as soon as she could walk. After she had been dancing for years, she was surprised and insulted when some visitors tried to teach her the steps that she already knew better than they did. She didn't need them to instruct her in swinging from hand to hand in the "beeg circle" at the end of the square dance Georg Bidstrup loved to call. Georg liked to call her the little red caboose as she brought up the end of the long line in her bright red dress!

LIFE CHANGES

As I had over the years, from time to time I worked in the Brasstown post office with Mrs. Green. Then I became so busy with the children, the garden, and farm work that I hadn't been able to work at the post office. I had always enjoyed staying in touch with community news by talking with people who came in to pick up their mail.

Monroe had been working at the Lidseen plant for almost ten years. Every morning he packed a lunch, filled his coffee thermos, and walked down to Old Highway 64 to catch a ride with fellow workers. Though he was comfortable with his work, Monroe was interested in changing jobs. When a quiet rumor whispered that Iowa Green was getting ready to retire and her Civil Service position would become a political plum, both of us pricked up our ears. For either Monroe or me, the job would certainly be good enough to dissolve the financial crunch small subsistence farming had put us in.

Quentin Moore, who had been postmaster in Hayesville for a number of years, explained for us the intricacies of securing a job with the federal government. The procedure was deliberate and politically influenced. We could prepare ourselves by studying the type of true-or-false questions that were usually asked on Civil Service exams. After the exam, the two North Carolina senators would name someone from the list of people who passed. If he approved, the President would confirm their choice. We were lifelong registered Democrats and our North Carolina senators were both Democrats. At this time Dwight Eisenhower, a Republican, was the president and would not appoint a Democrat. The choice would definitely be political, and the position would not be filled until after the presidential election in 1960.

Quentin thought Monroe would make a good postmaster and would enjoy the position. He also knew of my interest and suggested that both Monroe and I take the exam to increase our chances of success.Mrs. Green retired, and the legal and political process to fill her position began.

We both signed up to take the examination and were notified of the date it would be given. Monroe and I, and several other people from Brasstown, drove the sixty miles over to Sylva and took the exam. We held our breath, and finally the list of those who passed arrived. Monroe was the only veteran on the list and received extra points that put him at the top. I was second on the list, and Blanche Smith, our neighbor and another good Democrat, was third. Republicans who passed did not expect to be chosen because they would not be named by the Democrat senators. Therefore we three effectively formed the list of eligible candidates.

In 1960, Democrat John F. Kennedy was elected president. Soon after he was sworn into office, he appointed Monroe to be Brasstown's new postmaster. With Monroe's entrance into Civil Service, we no longer needed to depend on short-term jobs. Our subsequent years of enjoying country life in Brasstown were simpler years of cutting hay, growing fresh vegetables, milking the cow, gathering eggs, and butchering our own meat. How grateful we were that our money crunch was over.

Conveniently, the post office was right at the end of our driveway. Every afternoon Florence and I walked down with cookies and a thermos for a coffee break with Dad. When the school bus arrived later in the afternoon, the three older children stopped in to tell Dad the news of the day before heading up the hill for their cookies and milk and the TV shows they loved to watch after school.

We had been fortunate in having all the neighborhood children play with ours at our house for the past several years. By the time the school year started in 1964, all of our children except Florence were enrolled in Ogden School. She had completed preschool, there was no kindergarten, and she could not start first grade until she celebrated her sixth birthday in August. I wondered what she would do in the first grade next winter without academic challenge, after having me all to herself for a year.

Florence had begun recognizing signs and labels when we got our first television the year Danny started school. When we passed a service station, Florence recognized the Texaco sign because she had seen it nightly as we watched the Texaco Huntley-Brinkley Report. By the Christmas after her third birthday, she could read all the gift tags on family presents. Now at the age of five, Florence could pick up almost anything in print and read at least part of it. In the years before television was widespread, early readers were unusual. They were the subject of curiosity and considerable research. Dr. Stanley Nale, a psychologist from Western Carolina University recruited Florence for his research on early readers.

Several years after we bought the farm, a group of women in Murphy had organized a chapter of the American Association of University Women and invited me to join. I was delighted to know other college graduates and enjoyed the monthly meetings in members' homes. One evening in September I went to a committee planning meeting at the Folk School with three or four other members. My friend Mary Ressel had called the meeting to plan an endeavor we were contemplating for our chapter of AAUW. Mary had a husband who was in charge of a local assembly plant, five school-age children, and a full-time job as a social worker with the Department of Public Welfare in Murphy. She was also juggling the responsibility for this planning meeting that evening. Suddenly she stopped in midsentence and looked at me. "Why don't you take on half my job?" she asked. "I would really like to work only half the week. Wouldn't you like to do social work?"

"It is exactly what I would like to do, but I don't have a degree in social work, just in English literature."

"You don't need any special education for social work in Public Welfare. All that is required is a bachelor's degree from college and a passing grade on the State Merit Board Exam."

I was intrigued. If I went to work in Murphy, Florence could go with me and attend the private kindergarten classes being held at the Methodist church. So I replied, "Of course I'd love to do that. Do you really mean it?"

Mary assured me that she did. "I'll tell Vernie, my boss, in the morning. You can call him and tell him you're interested." The next morning I talked it over with Monroe and the children. If I had a job and made extra money, we could go on vacations and have other extras. The family agreed, and I made an appointment with Mr. Vernie Ayers, the director of the Welfare Department in Cherokee County, for the next afternoon.

The Welfare Department offices were on the second floor of the marble courthouse in Murphy. Florence and I walked up the steps into the courthouse, somewhat in awe of our unfamiliar surroundings. We climbed the open circular stairway the large rotunda to the second floor. Vernie was waiting for us behind the desk in his office, the command post. After removing a badly chewed cigar from his mouth, he gave me a crooked smile and rose to shake my hand. His bold turquoise eyes met mine. A troublesome tremor plagued his body, but his mind was wondrously alive.

"Mary Ressel tells me you are interested in sharing her position," he began and motioned me to a seat across the desk from him. Florence, her eyes wide with curiosity, climbed into my lap.

"I like working with people," I replied. "Family responsibilities take up much of my time, so a half-time position would be ideal for me too."

"You graduated from college?"

"Yes, Vassar. I majored in English, contemporary press, and social studies."

"Job experience?"

"Well, I worked at the Folk School for a year; then during the war I did a year of apprentice teaching in Cambridge, Massachusetts; and I taught junior high social studies in New York for two years. After coming here I taught seventh grade at Martins Creek School for a year. Other than that I've had a variety of short-term jobs that have given me some experience with people. Five years ago I was a secretary for the Clay County Extension office before our second child was born." I paused for a breath. "My husband and I farmed for seven years in Brasstown: dairy, pigs, and chickens before our family took up so much of our time and money," I said with a laugh.

"You'll need to take the State Merit Board Exam over in Sylva. I think they have one scheduled for next week. Then I'll have to get the results before I can hire you."

Vernie then became very businesslike. He waved his right hand over the thick books on his desk and toward the shelves of legal volumes beside him."These are our regulations and laws. Everything we do here is regulated by these books. We have three types of assistance. Old Age Assistance (OAA) is for people over sixty-five who worked before there was a Social Security system. They have to meet the eligibility requirements and show that their resources are limited to very little beyond their home. The same is true for the Adult Disabled (AD). For the dependent children who are without the support of one parent due to disability, desertion, or death there is assistance based on a monthly budget which we figure twice a year. All the regulations for eligibility and what we can do to help are outlined in these books."

"I see," I replied, impressed by the legality that seemed to be so familiar to Mr. Ayers.

"I want to go with you when you make your first home visits after you come to work. We determine eligibility here in the office, but we make a home visit also. Then we review the status yearly for the first two categories and twice a year for the families. I want to introduce you to the work and get you off on the right foot with these families."

That seemed to conclude the interview. Vernie showed us around the office, introducing me to secretaries and social workers. With a mingled sense of relief and excitement, Florence and I headed home filled with zeal for social work and President Lyndon Johnson's plan to eliminate poverty in this great country of ours.

SOCIAL WORKER I

The next week I took the State Merit Board Exam in Sylva. As soon as I heard from Mr. Ayers that I had passed and been hired, I enrolled Florence in kindergarten at the Murphy Methodist church. I would be working Monday, Tuesday, and Wednesday in the morning, and on Thursday and Friday I'd be working in the afternoons. Florence would be at school for the mornings, and my friend Jewell Rogers in Brasstown agreed to take care of her for the two afternoons each week. I was ready to start my career as a "Social Worker I" for the North Carolina Department of Public Welfare.

On the Monday morning I started work, I took Florence to kindergarten before I went to my office. She was met at the car by a little girl Sara Wells, who had appointed herself a welcoming committee of one when we went to enroll. Walking toward the entrance to kindergarten, Sara pointed to a sign over the water fountain and said logically and proudly, "That says, 'Water fountain.'"

"No," Florence corrected, "it says Men's Bible Class."

Needless to say, a five-year-olds argument erupted. Finally a teacher appeared and settled the disagreement, as amazed at Florence's reading skill as was Sara. Then I left Florence to deal with the kindergarten world by herself.

At the office, Vernie was as good as his word. He spent the mornings of my first week orienting me as to what I would be expected to do with a client who came to the office to apply for assistance. On Thursday I left Florence at Jewell's house to spend the afternoon. At the office I collected the necessary forms and applications I would need for the afternoon's home visits and careful directions to each home we had scheduled. I was ready for my first expedition into the field.

Vernie wanted me to drive so I would get acquainted with the territory. Early on he had been the only social worker in the county, so he knew all the back roads and many of the people: welfare recipients, town fathers, and government officials. Although he sat on the passenger side of my station wagon he was genuinely in the driver's seat in all other respects.

We headed out of Murphy down Tennessee Street, past the movie theater, across the bridge over Valley River, and out Joe Brown Highway toward Unaka. The narrow, two-lane paved road wound twenty miles through back country past Hiwassee Lake and Grape Creek to the community of Unaka before looping back through Boiling Springs, Hanging Dog, Ebenezer, Bates Creek, and back to Murphy. Vernie pointed out the landmarks, churches, and stores where I could ask for directions and houses I might visit later.

In that part of the county many of the men supplemented subsistence farming by cutting and selling pine pulpwood that would be shipped out of Murphy by rail to paper mills. They drove old trucks loaded to capacity, often with tires worn slick with wear. Traffic was light and those who regularly drove the Joe Brown Highway thought they owned the road. Vernie warned me that defensive driving was always called for if you didn't want a head-on collision far from home.

The day that Vernie showed me my territory, we stopped first in Unaka. Unaka was a tiny collection of houses, an elementary school, a general store and gas station, a couple of churches, and a six-by-six-foot post office. It was the center of a small farming community and had not yet been discovered by "furriners." Off a gravel road beyond the tiny post office, we came to a porchless, weatherbeaten house set back from the road in the midst of fields of ripe corn and somewhat overgrazed pasture. There were a few old out buildings and a barn with sticks of tobacco leaves hanging to dry.

Vernie directed me to turn the car around and park it ready to drive out. "It's always a good idea to turn around before you go in for your visit. If you get stuck, then the family you are visiting can help push you out. Some of these places are pretty rough. I never sit in an upholstered chair. They're apt to be nasty. Pick a good clean place before you sit down."

We knocked and waited. A tired-looking woman with a small girl clinging to her skirt opened the door. "Good afternoon, Mrs. Jones," said Vernie politely, "I've brought Mrs. Wilson here with me to do your six-month review. She's our new social worker who will be visiting you."

I nodded, smiled, and murmured a greeting, but followed Vernie's lead and shook hands lightly. Mrs. Jones led us from the dark entry hall of the old two-story house into a side room that served as living space. On the open hearth of a crude piled-stone fireplace a trash pile was smoldering. The lady of the house sat beside it and shifted her lip of snuff to spit in the fireplace before speaking. "Just find yourself a place to sit. I've been feeling poorly and hain't got the house cleaned up yit," she apologized.

Vernie chose a straight chair and I sat on the front edge of another. Two small children were playing jacks on the bare wooden floor. A third little girl sat straight legged on a sagging sofa, hugging a live chicken to her breast. "Are the other children in school today?" Vernie asked. He had explained that the headcount must always be verified before the budget could be figured.

Mrs. Jones's tired face brightened a bit. "Julie's in the sixth this year and Gordon's in the fourth. This one should be in the second, but she was feeling poorly this morning, so I just kept her out. The other two just stay with me all the time so I can't get a thing done around the house. They're too little to help much."

The room was cluttered with clothes scattered everywhere. A box by the hearth held a brood of chicks. The mother hen left the sanctuary of the small girl's arms and hopped across the floor to settle protectively over her chicks. The woman watched the amazement that flooded my face and felt a need to explain."That broody hen chose a queer time to set and hatch a brood of young ones. We had to bring her to the house to save them from the fox. Now Julie and the little ones have made a pet of her."

With that remark both children left their game of jacks and began to quarrel over the hen, pulling her off the chicks, their bare feet slipping on the droppings that covered the floor in patches. Their mother raised her hand, threatening them without a word. They sat down with the mother hen clutched between them.

We proceeded with the interview. "Does Mr. Jones plan to sell the tobacco in Asheville this year? . . . Has his health improved any?" Vernie queried, asking questions one at a time and giving the woman plenty of time to answer. "He'll need to get this medical form filled out by his doctor, you know."

"Yes sir, Doc Lewis says he'll never get shed of that TB. We'll take that form and get him to fill that out for you. Dr. Lewis is the one who sees most of us down this way, but it means a trip into town."

Having thus covered the need to verify eligibility, Vernie went over the budgeted allowances for a family of seven. With Mrs. Jones's agreement, he estimated fuel costs above the wood cut on the place, looked at light bills, and deducted the value of the garden produce they raised, as well as the probable income from the tobacco sale. "Now if there are any changes in the family, or you need help with anything, you just call Mrs. Wilson. She'll be back to see you. Do you have any questions about the check?"

"No sir, Mr. Ayers. We shore are obliged. Don't know what we'd do without your help. Come back any time." We rose and she went with us to the door.

As we drove away, I asked, "Is that a typical home?"

"There is really no such thing as typical," Vernie assured me. "These folks are perhaps a little worse off than some. She's weak and he's sick, but I guess they do the best they can with what they've got."

We drove on over the mountain toward Boiling Springs and turned off on a small side road toward Ebenezer. There was a confusing maze of narrow gravel roads, identified only by the state road number in black on a small white sign affixed to a low post, but Vernie knew each twist and turn. We reached a narrow, deeply shaded curve beside a sloping granite hill that came right down to the road. He directed me to pull over on the left side in front of a tiny cabin perched beside the rock. The house hung between the road and a dense rhododendron thicket that reached up the side of the mountain out of sight.

"This is where Miss Mamie has lived all her life," Vernie told me. We got out of the car and climbed up the open steps to her wide porch. It was a steep climb, and I marveled at Vernie's ability to do it and at the indomitable spirit he had in his crippled body. He knocked loudly on the heavy hand-hewn wooden door. After a minute it swung open on leather hinges. Miss Mamie greeted us graciously. She was dressed in a long, bright calico dress covered neatly with a starched, white apron made from bleached flour sacks.

"Come in, Mr. Ayers, it is good to see you. I was hoping for your visit today."

The small front room was dark. There were two high windows, one on each side of the front door. A Warm Morning heater took up one corner of the room that was furnished with a comfortable armchair, a willow rocker, a small table, two straight chairs, and a pie safe set against the wall. Through an open door I could see a high four-poster bed. In a side room there was a tiny kitchen with an oil lamp set on a wall shelf. In the living room an Aladdin lamp hung over the small table.

"Well, Miss Mamie, I see you still don't have electricity. Have you had that spring water piped down into your kitchen?"

"No sir, I haven't. I just step across that big flat rock outside and up to where the spring comes out of the rock. You can see it trickling down out there. It's worn a groove in the side of the stone, it's been there so long. It's handy for me, and the water's real good and cold and fresh."

"Well, it would be easier for you in bad weather. It wouldn't cost much at all to get that pipe put in. We could add it into your budget as an essential improvement, and you'd never notice the cost."

"It might not taste as good. I don't need that. I've toted water all my life. Wouldn't know what to do with myself without that night chore. Thank you kindly anyway, Mr. Ayers."

We chatted a while with her in that cozy little room, bringing her a taste of life away from her immediate environment and news to share with the neighbors who visited her frequently. Her small check each month gave her a sense of security and self-worth and made it possible for her to take care of herself as she moved through the decade of her seventies.

When we returned to the car, Vernie told me Miss Mamie's history. She had never married. She cared for her parents in this house until they died several years ago. After she used up all their savings, she did without much of everything that most folks think are essential, until a cousin applied for Old Age Assistance for her. It was difficult to get her to accept "charity." She had never worked outside the home, and there was no Social Security. Finally she had the flu one winter, and the necessity for a doctor persuaded her that she needed help. She was now probably the most conservative and appreciative recipient of Old Age Assistance in the state of North Carolina.

We left Miss Mamie and drove on to Bates Creek where we visited a young man born with cerebral palsy. He lived with his parents and spent most of his time in a rough, handmade wheelchair on the front porch of their house watching the country traffic move back and forth on the narrow paved road in front of their place. Speech was difficult for Richard. He grimaced his greeting and listened as we talked with his mother about his condition.

"He seems to be doing all right," she said. "I hardly ever have to take him to the doctor. He's such a good-natured fellow, never complains, likes to watch the cars and listen to the radio. I don't know what I'd do without his company."

There was no question of Richard's eligibility for assistance. His parents did well to take care of him and themselves at home with minimal opportunities to grow their own food or to pick up odd jobs for neighbors in their spare time. They were cheerful and cooperative—part of what others thought of as the deserving poor. They genuinely needed Richard's AD check to enable them to take care of him.

That visit finished our afternoon of reviews. Vernie seemed pleased that I had taken it all in stride. On my part, I was fascinated with the opportunity to meet these people whose paths in life were so different from my own. I looked forward to more of this work in the war against poverty.

The next week I had my initial interview application in the office. A slim, young black woman came in to apply for assistance on behalf of her four small children whose father had deserted them all for a job in Ohio. I immediately felt a connection with her. Four children? Yes, I know about that. What in the world would I have done when they were all small if Monroe had left me?

She filled out the information on the form without any difficulty and invited me to come for a visit in Texana where she lived across from the elementary school. Texana was the section of Murphy across the river where most of the black people lived at that time. I had never been there. It was easy to bypass that community on the way west on Joe Brown Highway.

When she left, I asked Vernie if I was allowed to go for a home visit. "Of course, that's the best part. You'll spend most of your time in the field, making home visits. It's essential for a new application. You need to verify what she has told you by seeing the house and the children and by looking at her bills so you can make a budget with her."

With her clear directions, I didn't have any trouble finding her home. Two little boys were sitting on the front steps. They moved over as I walked up to knock on the door, but they hid their faces when I said, "Good morning." I knocked and a voice called, "Come in."

"Gloria," I called. (She had asked me to call her by her first name.) She was hanging out one of the windows trying to fasten a screen. As I greeted her, she came down out of the window and came toward me saying, "I'm just fixing this house so we won't have flies." Picking up a chair, she invited me to go back out to the yard where we could talk and get some air.

"Someone had thrown these screens in the dump and I pulled them out. They need mending, but they fit my windows pretty well," she explained. "I find a lot of useful things in the dump. Other people don't need them."

"I came to see where you live and see the other children. We need to get acquainted and figure your budget," I explained.

"The two littlest ones are napping," she said. We looked at her light bills and estimated her grocery and heating expenses. Then I asked her about her husband's whereabouts.

"Oh, we're not married. I met him in Asheville while I was in high school and staying with relatives there. You see there's no black high school in Murphy, and I wanted an education," she explained. "I was raised here and my mother is here, so when my boyfriend and I were having a hard time making ends meet in Asheville he decided he had to go to Ohio to get a good job. I came back here."

"Well, how much does he send you each week?"

"He hasn't sent me anything, and he probably won't. We're not married and its hard to save anything up there in Ohio. I just have to manage on my own. I love my kids."

I checked on the sleeping babies and wished her good luck. It would probably be temporary assistance, I thought. I was right. She called in a few months to tell me that he had come for her, and they were going to Ohio. I wished them well wherever they finally decided to settle down. I was thankful for knowing that her life proved that many of the stereotypical labels that people throw out carelessly are really untrue and unfair. This woman was neither lazy nor dirty nor ignorant, and her word was dependable.

Soon I made another home visit to a family with six children, They lived a short way out of town on a hill. I parked my car at the end of the rutted road that led there and walked up a worn path to the house. The trail was steep and it was raining, but I had an umbrella. I was in good shape, but a bit pooped by the steep climb. When I reached the house that was set on piles about six feet above the ground, I found several old steps leading up to a front door. A bit winded, I knocked; the door flew open. The house was just one room and the family was at home.

"Mrs. Bole, I'm Mrs. Wilson from the Welfare Office. They say you called and needed to see me." My introduction caused a small flurry of excitement in the children, but the plump lady rose quickly from the sagging sofa and came toward me.

"It's my husband," Mrs. Bole explained."He's gone to try to find us a better house. I don't know what to do because he hasn't come back or called. The older children are both in school, and I can't do anything with these young'uns." She found a straight chair, wiped it off casually for me, and told the child who was sitting there glumly to go and sit in the corner. Cans were placed in strategic spots around the floor to catch leaks from holes in the roof. Children were lying on makeshift pallets here and there. The floor was muddy, and everything seemed in need of a good scrubbing.

"Where do you get your water?" I asked.

"There's a good spring at the bottom of the hill," she said, "but we can't tote enough up the path to wash anything. The outhouse is down there too, and the young'uns are afraid to go down by theirselves. They just use the knot holes in the floor. I was hoping to catch enough water in these cans to wash up a bit. Do you know of any house we could get these days?"

"I'm sorry, I don't know of one right now, but we'll be on the lookout and maybe your husband is finding a better place today." I tried to sound cheerful, but I thought of the people who said so carelessly, "Well, at least they could stay clean even if they are on welfare!" It would seem impossible under these conditions. I remembered how difficult cleanliness was when we went camping and how accustomed to dirt we became after a few days!

"Do you have enough here to eat, Mrs. Bole?" I asked.

"We have some crackers and peanut butter still."

"Do you have folks close by?"

"No ma'am, but he does."

"Would they help you until he finds a house?"

"I don't know, ma'am; they're not close."

"How about neighbors? I think you need help until your husband finds another place for you all. Can you tell me his folks' name and telephone number? Perhaps I could call them and tell them that you need help until he gets back. Would you let me do that for you?"

She hesitated, but then dug a scrap of wrinkled paper out of her pocket and gave it to me. There was little more I could do to help this family, but I stayed a while and listened to her complaints and worries and tried as best I could to leave some hope with her. Back at the office I called the husband's parents and talked with them about the need of a safe home for their grandchildren until their son could find a place for them to move. I think they managed to take food and to get in touch with their son who was having difficulties of his own.

I traveled all over the western half of Cherokee County and met many families who were in need of help. There was one small house where the west wind blew through so freely that I shivered for them even when I was home and the west wind blew through our pine trees signaling colder weather to come. Often there was not much I could do but assure them of the monthly check and the food stamps to which their circumstances entitled them. Most people did the best they could with the situation in which they found themselves, and I learned something of value from each person.

Over the years in Cherokee, Clay, and Graham counties, I worked with families I will never forget. Sometimes I spent so much time with a family that I came to care almost too much. Most of the women were culturally inclined to be dependent, but they were resourceful and fiercely protective of their children.

I became very respectful of one family that I worked with for several years. The father had a serious addiction to alcohol and was periodically imprisoned for behavior related to that. The mother was a good manager and resourceful, but when she became seriously ill, she waited too long for treatment. When I went to see her in the hospital, the children were scattered among older married siblings and other relatives in an adjoining state, but she knew that they needed to be together to support each other and begged my help in achieving that. With the assistance of a church-related foster home system in Charlotte, we found foster parents who cared for the smallest members of the family until they were old enough to be reunited with the others. They also knew that I cared about them and that when they needed advice or help they could, and did, get in touch with me. I was happy to be able to see them grow up successfully.

There was a great deal of sadness in the work, but satisfaction as well. Someone stopped me one morning as I came out of a hospital visit and said. "Don't you ever get tired of hearing about everyone's troubles ?" I replied, "Honestly I don't. I am thankful each time someone trusts me enough to tell me the truth of their situation and allow me to try to help. When anyone shares their own story with me, I feel enriched by their experience."Being asked that question made me think of all the people from whom I had learned so much.

A good many mothers tolerated abusive husbands rather than raise their children without a father. Many others brought up their children alone after death or desertion. One mother I knew walked a mile down the mountain from her house every afternoon to meet the school bus and walk back to the house with three teenage daughters, rather than risk their molestation by an unsupervised relative.

I learned much from some about managing a small income carefully, and I also taught many by sharing my personal experiences. Fathers were sometimes open to working on conversational skills and improving their understanding of a woman's role and work. Understanding the man's point of view gave me a better perspective when advising his wife.

With the end of the decade of the sixties my work with these families came to an end, and I worked in a more structured environment for ten years until my retirement in 1982. I believe that Lyndon Johnson's War on Poverty and other programs had beneficial effects in the late sixties. Many situations in our area have improved in the years since I was visiting families who received welfare assistance. In our section of the mountains we have established resources for abused women and for handicapped workers who may now receive companionship, training, recreation, and work at Industrial Opportunities, Inc. There is a community college offering training in a number of professions. There are many more jobs of all kinds available. There is better housing. Churches have multiplied in number and have increased the scope of their ministries.

I am deeply appreciative of the many people I came to know and all they taught me about their lives that I would never have known without their trust and willingness to share their stories. However, I am even more appreciative of Monroe's patience with the long hours I spent working.

THE SEVENTIES AND BEYOND

During the decade of the 1970s, Monroe worked as the Brasstown postmaster, and our children were finishing school and starting off to college. I continued to work with individuals and families who were deprived in ways that made them eligible for public assistance from the state. I had found their circumstances interesting and understandable. I especially liked working with parents who were struggling to bring up children to be independent, contributing members of the community, but I liked working with any mother who cared more for her children than for her independence.

Even though there were more medical facilities than previously, public transportation was minimal, making it difficult for many people to visit doctors or treatment centers. As a result, when I made referrals to clinics and specialized hospitals at a moderate distance away, I needed to provide transportation. Thankfully my social service director always approved my requests for an additional mileage allowance.

Even as I started work with these families, I had recognized many individuals whose needs were not being met. There were occasional patients with mild psychological problems; children with learning, hearing, and visual difficulties; and various situations that county health nurses could not treat effectively. As county health departments began to have greater financial resources, more centralized clinics were established. A specialized clinic for congenital heart problems was opened in Sylva, only half the distance to facilities in Asheville, and it was not limited to the impoverished.

At this time Western Carolina University in Cullowhee began graduating master level psychologists and sending them to other counties to do school testing and other diagnostic tests of both children and adults who needed treatment. As a result, several families in Cherokee County came together to form a support group made up of friends and relatives caring for individuals with handicaps of any kind. They named the group We Care and met regularly to discuss solutions for the mentally, physically, or emotionally disadvantaged people for whom they cared. The Methodist church offered a vacant house they owned in Marble for meetings of the group. A graduate psychologist from Cullowhee traveled over on Monday nights to teach a class of volunteers.

A number of social workers in several surrounding counties joined these classes. A wonderful psychiatrist in Franklin, Dr. Amelia Kahn, joined psychologist Dr. Ben Monroe to recruit a board of directors from a five-county area in the southwestern mountains of North Carolina. They organized an association of psychologists with a central office in Dillsboro. This was the beginning of the Smoky Mountain Area Mental Health Center. As locations became available, they opened centers and provided services in the county health offices for the treatment of psychological problems.

The We Care group in Cherokee County readied the donated house in Marble—cleaning, repairing, painting, and furnishing. Volunteers staffed the office and began seeing people who came for help. Linda Kennedy, a psychiatric social worker, was the first part-time director, but Dr. Peter Cook soon became the director.

Dr. Cook visited the Departments of Social Services, Health Departments, and school districts in Cherokee, Clay, and Graham counties to explain the services that would be available from the Marble Center. When the center opened, Dr. Cook and one other psychologist were the only therapists available to see clients who sought treatment. Many people in our area were bashful about seeking help, afraid of psychologists, and reluctant to talk about personal problems; but they were also curious. Dr. Cook was an outgoing, fun-loving person; and was well educated, caring, and interested in people. However, he and the other therapist had a limited amount of time for hourly interviews. They needed another staff member ready to welcome and complete intake information for those who came to find treatment. After meeting me in Brasstown, they recognized that as a long-term resident, I was acquainted with many people in the community. They believed that I could put people at ease, so after examining my credentials during an interview in Cullowhee, I became the third staff member at the Marble Mental Health Center in Cherokee County.

I was adept at taking personal histories, and I loved meeting new people. These were unfamiliar clients, wanting to be better understood. It was fun to help people uncover whatever was worrying them. (I was reminded of the delight I had taken in college chemistry when we went through the process of finding the components of an unknown material.)

Each week in staff meeting, I presented the intakes of the week with a brief social history. Therapists gave short progress reports on the clients they had seen and sometimes asked for consultation from the group. A therapist was assigned to each new client.

At these staff meetings we also interviewed applicants for the position of children and youth psychologist in each of the three counties that the Marble Center covered. Those counselors would each be furnished with a pickup truck outfitted as an office in which to travel from rural school to school. The back of the truck had been converted to serve as a miniature classroom, complete with a table and chairs, bookcases, file drawers; as well as a blackboard and books, puzzles, and games. One of these youth psychologists later became my good friend, ally, and partner. He had been working as a psychologist with inmates in a long-term prison and had recently moved with his family to the area. When I asked if he had experience with children he replied honestly, "Not very much, but my wife and I are expecting our second child, and I expect I will soon have lots of experience!"

In the beginning, the five-county professional staff of Smoky Mountain Area Mental Health gathered for regular training sessions to teach and study developing methods of dealing with various specialties of our work. We met in different centrally located schools and town halls and formed cooperative relationships with each other. We also worked alongside Dr. Kahn and the other psychiatrists who succeeded her in her retirement. Each maintained the practice of always being available to us for consultation and advice about clients with whom we were working. For me it was an invaluable education.

As years went on, my work was concentrated on couples and families. I repeatedly taught parenting classes and spoke on communication styles and customs. Soon after I began work at the Marble Center, I became involved with a program in Cherokee County for individuals who were too handicapped to go the work.

Ann Golem from Andrews was very interested in such a program and was supported by her Catholic priest, Father Tom Meehan. Ann was a caring mother of a young man who had attended school in a northern state where there was much discrimination toward people with disabilities and very little appropriate education was offered. The family had recently moved to Andrews, and Ann knew that her son was capable of learning more than he had achieved in school and of forming good relationships with people near to his age. She also felt that he needed a great deal more independence from his caring family.

I knew of other people who could profit from and enjoy a "sheltered workshop." A group of leaders in Marble offered their community center across from the Marble Mental Health Center as a place where we could meet. Their use of the meeting place was mostly on weekends or in the evenings. So we selected a time and day and notified interested people in the area of our hopes and plans to meet and organize such a workshop.

The day was cold and cloudy as we gathered. Among the first to arrive were Barry and Robin Wheeler, a couple from the Teachers Corps in Ohio, who had recently come to the Folk School to live while they sought work in their field of occupational teaching and special education. A young man from Western Carolina University in Cullowhee finishing his master's degree program in special education was there, as was a Methodist minister from Murphy, Frank Turner.

We gathered and talked, and were thankful this group. There was no doubt of the need for a program to provide employment to severely handicapped individuals. The young man from Cullowhee offered to direct and teach a group for the first year free of charge, as part of his practicum. Frank Turner offered to pick up clients in Cherokee County in his station wagon. Ann Golem offered transportation from Andrews. We discussed starting dates and agreed that there was no time like the present. The organization that was to become Industrial Occupations, Inc. (IOI) was born.

Soon after this meeting, Gretchen and Bob Fink joined the staff at Marble Mental Health Center, and the following year Bob became director of the sheltered workshop. He moved the group to the large, and now empty, Ogden School building, which afforded plenty of space for machinery to build simple projects. Bob set up a working schedule that won approval from the workers and the community. With leadership and assistance from many sources, IOI has grown and thrives to this day.

At the Marble Mental Health Center, Mary Ricketson and I were the therapists for families and groups. We met often with women who were having difficulties with abusive spouses. It was hard to advise them with no resources or protection in the community. The police were often uncooperative, placing the responsibility on the women and advising them only that they should not provoke trouble.

Mary contacted female personnel directors at the nearby plants and invited them to meet with us in Murphy to assess the need for a battered women's shelter. We drove to Murphy to meet with a group during our lunch hour on Mondays. When the group increased in numbers, we moved the meetings to the library in Andrews. It was at the first advertised meeting there that I met Robin Mauney, a senior at Western Carolina University. She was majoring in sociology and doing a thesis on this problem. Basically she took the ball and ran with it. The REACH center was opened in a protected, deserted house, its location kept secret. It has grown and expanded for more than thirty years, a model for other protective homes with services for mountain-area individuals abused in domestic relationships.

During the decade of the seventies, in my free time I furthered my expertise by taking one course at a time at Western Carolina University. In 1979, I completed a master's degree in nonschool counseling.

Then, in 1981, the state of North Carolina revised the state budget. Mental health funds were reduced to the extent that Smoky Mountain Area Mental Health was forced to make a reduction of staff. The director asked for staff members to consider resignation. I had worked ten years at the Marble Center and, at that time, finished a total of twenty years working with the state of North Carolina in my various professions—teaching, social service, and mental health.

Throughout the time I worked at the Smoky Mountain Area Mental Health Center, Monroe continued to serve as postmaster in Brasstown. Our children completed their college experiences. Danny, Anne, John, and Florence were busy doing many interesting things in different places. Keeping up with their lives could be a full-time job in itself, and the time seemed right to satisfy my desire for travel. I volunteered to resign.

EPILOGUE

After I retired from the Smoky Mountain Area Mental Health Center in Marble, a long-time friend, who was a psychologist, opened a private counseling service with me in the basement office of my home. Monroe furnished his woodworking shop in the barn, looking toward retirement from the post office.

Danny had tried a year at Montreat-Anderson College near Asheville and decided he would rather hitchhike wherever he wanted to go and could support himself by working in fast-food restaurants. He had jobs all over North Carolina before graduating to private restaurants. Then, in 1984, Danny found his niche working at Murphy Medical Hospital.

Anne graduated from the University of Tennessee in Knoxville and worked there for several years before going to Salt Lake City, Utah, to get her masters degree in social work. She graduated, married, and returned east to work in Massachusetts. We enjoyed visiting her in both locations.

John and Florence both graduated from the University of the South in Sewanee, Tennessee. John married, then completed his doctorate in mathematics at the University of North Carolina at Chapel Hill. John teaches at Centre College in Danville, Kentucky. Florence stayed in Sewanee to work for two years before moving home for a year and then on to Birmingham, Alabama. She completed her master's degree in clinical nutrition from the University of Alabama in Birmingham, where she met her husband who is a pulmonary physician. They now live in Pittsburgh, Pennsylvania.

Our adult children's activities and moves kept Monroe and me busy just trying to keep up with them all. For several years we attended all sorts of graduation events, then concentrated on visiting our sons and daughters, who were establishing homes and having babies—six fine grandchildren who are all now teenagers.

Monroe felt he had seen enough of the world while in the navy, but I was excited to use my newly established retirement compensation from Smoky Mountain Area Mental Health to take a trip to England with Florence and John and his wife, Brenda. We stayed at bed-and-breakfasts; and, using rail passes, traveled to London, Dover, Oxford, and Cambridge in England. We visited Edinburgh, Scotland, and towns along the west coast of Wales. It was the trip I had wanted to take all my life, and I'd happily take it again!

The next year I traveled to France with my friend Jacques Marchat, his wife, and three ladies from Atlanta. He rented a station wagon in Brussels and then drove us all around France on secondary roads. We stayed in small hotels along the way. We then drove from Geneva, Switzerland, down the Rhone Valley. We stayed for a week in Avignon exploring the Mediterranean coast, then went back to Paris for several days before flying home.

My last trip overseas was a cultural exchange trip to the Soviet Union in the early 1980s. It also was a great experience, perhaps especially so because I shared it with my cousin Adele. Back in Brasstown, I mentored Education for Ministry courses, was honored by the Diocese of Western North Carolina as a Distinguished Communicant, and traveled back and forth to Asheville on diocesan business.

In 1995, Monroe and I celebrated our fiftieth wedding anniversary in Radford, Virginia, a central location chosen so that our four children and their families could all share the event with us. A year later, Monroe died in October. I still live half the year in our home in Brasstown, with Danny and many friends nearby. In Danville, Kentucky, I have also settled into a small home near John and Brenda. I spend part of each year there making new friends, writing, and establishing new hobbies.